DIGITAL CHILDREN

A GUIDE FOR ADULTS

SANDRA LEATON GRAY

AND

ANDY PHIPPEN

First Published 2021

by John Catt Educational Ltd,
15 Riduna Park, Station Road,
Melton, Woodbridge IP12 1QT

Tel: +44 (0) 1394 389850
Email: enquiries@johncatt.com
Website: www.johncatt.com

ISBN: 978 1 913622 81 7

Set and designed by John Catt Educational Limited

Reviews

Leaton Gray and Phippen provide the arguments and analysis that will help adults make discerned choices in supporting children's digital lives – a resource that is so precious in the confusing territory of children's media use. From issues such as online safety, through sexting to artificial intelligence, the authors cover the challenges and possibilities of children's lives in the digital era. They do not shy away from controversial topics and frankly portray ongoing research debates within the framework of four different models of childhood. Drawing on rigorous research and lively vignettes, this highly accessible book will appeal to all parents and caregivers interested in the complex issues of digital childhoods.

Natalia Kucirkova is Professor of Early Childhood Education and Development at the University of Stavanger in Norway, Professor of Reading and Children's Development at The Open University and Visiting Professor at University College London in the UK.

The world has changed dramatically for children in the last few decades. Parents and carers are often struggling to work out the best way to respond – is the digital world a threat to their child, or an opportunity? How should they balance allowing their child to explore freely with safety? This thought-provoking book should help them make the best decisions.

Julian Huppert is the Director of the Intellectual Forum at Jesus College, Cambridge University. He is a former MP and member of the Home Affairs Select Committee.

Acknowledgements

We would like to thank our parents, for their forbearance over the years, and our children, for their patience (and stories).

Contents

Foreword

The pace of societal change has exposed a gap between parents and their children. Many parents are perplexed by the challenges of relating to their children's digital universe. Authorities and the mainstream media have often reacted with moral panic or endorsed technological and legal solutions like filtering and child monitoring, the latter of which often approaches intrusive surveillance, all in the interests of children's safety.

To deal with this, the authors have taken a common-sense and appropriately sceptical analysis to the myths that swirl around the question of young people's digital and physical safety. For example, they show that a child is more likely to be injured on the road, around the house or on a backyard trampoline than be groomed and kidnapped through online activity.

This is a book that also provides a clear guide to the occasionally complex world of digital technologies. Biometrics, encryption, ciphertext and sexting, all are explained and their relevance to young people analysed. The authors raise a number of critical questions about the lives of young people and their relationship with digital technologies such as games, social media and tracking devices. Just as important are the questions raised about the potential dangers of society relying far too much on technology, rather than fostering relationships in which people work together or innovate or socialise. The key question for them is about the quality of conversations between parents and their kids, not prohibition or surveillance.

As a former Education Minister in Australia and the now the Chair of the international Biometrics Institute, I was astonished at the degree to which, in some countries, young people are measured, assessed and reported on throughout their school lives. Much of this is done using digital technologies and the authors are correct in asserting that the reporting and oversight regimes can have a number of deleterious effects. Out go human observation and connection, in come standardised tests, the (often cheap or sub-standard) biometrics to control library borrowing or school lunches, artificial intelligence which can monitor student inattention, and the gathering of personal data that can be misinterpreted or abused in later life.

Leaton Gray and Phippen are not Luddites, but they have sent up a warning flare as even the pet-shop parrot is trying to sell technology as the ultimate determinant of how we and our children should live and stay safe.

Terry Aulich is a former Senator and State Education Minister in Australia. He is Chair of the international Biometrics Institute's Privacy Expert Group.

Prologue

Our book may look familiar to some readers. This is because in 2017, we published another book, *Invisibly Blighted: The digital erosion of childhood*, which was aimed at an academic audience, addressing some of the key aspects of the digital age that were influencing the lives of children at the time (the title was derived from the Henry James horror novella *The Turn of the Screw*. We felt a connection as the novella explores the ambiguity of childhood innocence in a way that we felt reflected the confusion surrounding children and the internet today). We were subsequently invited by John Catt Publishers to create a popular version for a wider audience, which we have been delighted to do. The time span of four years is a long time in the digital world and has allowed us to update the subject matter extensively. It has also given us the opportunity to express ourselves in a more personal and immediate way than is usually possible within the rest of our academic lives, and has allowed us to lay out some of the complexities of the digital childhoods debate in a way that we hope will help and support those involved with the care and nurturing of children.

This book is designed to be read in a few sittings and inform readers about the latest debates surrounding controversial issues such as online safety, computer gaming, sexting, surveillance and monitoring, biometrics and artificial intelligence as they relate to children's lives in 2021. We have tried to make it particularly parent-friendly, because it seems to us that our fellow parents are pulled very many ways at the moment in relation to children's upbringing. Sometimes it seems that whatever they try to do is right and wrong at the same time. We have tried to provide material here that will allow parents to feel they are making more considered decisions about their children's digital lives, with greater understanding, and we've provided research referencing, so that readers can judge the quality of the information provided and follow new leads that might be of interest.

Before we launch into the main body of the book, however, we'd like to start with a short quiz, and we'll offer a similar quiz at the end of the book so readers can reflect on whether their views have altered.

Quiz

1. How would you mostly define children?

    A. Smaller versions of adults

    B. Vulnerable beings

    C. Innocents, a blank slate

    D. Creatures requiring civilising

    E. A lifestyle choice

2. How risky is it to be a child?

    A. Things are getting more dangerous for children compared to 1950.

    B. Things are getting safer for children compared to 1950.

3. Which of these represents the biggest risk for children at the moment?

    A. Online witchcraft sites

    B. Video gaming

    C. Being attacked or abducted by strangers

    D. Obesity

    E. Online pornography

    F. Drugs

    G. Radicalisation

    H. Personal data being stolen

    I. Covid-19

    J. Cars

    K. Back garden trampolines

4. Which is the most dangerous internet phenomenon?

    A. Blue Whale Challenge

B. Momo Challenge

C. Slenderman

D. *Doki Doki Literature Club*

5. Which has the biggest impact on children's wellbeing?

A. Eating breakfast regularly

B. Limiting screen time

Chapter 1
What is childhood anyway?

Sandra in her grandparents' garden

On the windowsill in Sandra's study at home there is a framed black and white photograph of her as a toddler in about 1970, pottering around contentedly in her grandparents' garden near Munich. She is wearing a little cotton dress and lace-up boots, smiling enigmatically to herself, pushing a miniature wheelbarrow across the grass. This is one of a series of photographs taken of Sandra over a couple of summers, where she was engaged earnestly in various everyday tasks. One striking thing about the series is that although there we can see a lot of small versions of adult equipment in evidence, toys feature relatively infrequently, even though her grandmother had made sure there were various fluffy animals, dolls, jumping jacks and toy bricks in the nursery (Sandra was the oldest grandchild on both sides and hence did quite well on the toy front, with many of the same playthings still doing duty for her own children). Another striking thing is that Sandra can remember many of the photographs being taken, and the thoughts going through her head at the time. Laying down memories so early and retaining them decades later is a little unusual, and there is a large body of published research literature on the whys and wherefores of how this might happen, and whether it is linked to early speech development, which is beyond the scope of what we are planning for this book. But for Sandra, there's the odd sensation of watching a film in her head of the event happening, while at the same time recalling the internal monologue that was going on at the same time. So what was she thinking?

At the age of two and a half, the toddler Sandra clearly saw herself as a prototype adult. She knew she was physically smaller than the people in her family (her brother would only arrive a couple of years later) but she saw herself as an apprentice version of these adults in her life, and remembers feeling driven to copy the things that she saw them doing. The wheelbarrow moment is quite vivid. On the one hand, Sandra knew that the wheelbarrow was completely empty, that much was obvious to her. On the other hand she could imagine the rich cornucopia of potential that might be sitting in the same wheelbarrow, if she were only an adult. The adult world was one of possibility and completeness, something to strive towards. Pottering about the garden happily as her grandmother planted out sweet peas meant she could be accepted as part of that world – one of the team.

What Sandra didn't know, of course, was that educationalists such as Maria Montessori (1870-1952) and Friedrich Fröbel (1782-1852) fully understood this 'apprenticeship' aspect of being a child, and indeed set up educational programmes to help the process along. Fröbel developed not only the concept of the kindergarten (children's garden) as a place of learning, but also a system of 'gifts' for children, such as woollen shapes and small bricks suited to chubby little fingers, aimed at helping them along a path of progression from a vague to a more definite understanding of the world (for example, building small models according to Fröbel's instruction sheets).

Fröbel's 'gifts' (Source: Wikimedia Commons) – these would have been given in stages to a small child, with instructions on the best manner of using them

Montessori, on the other hand, devised classroom routines for her pupils that were grounded in gently and systematically absorbing the knowledge and classification systems common to adult life, with coloured bricks and rods to line up and stack, and little trays along low shelves, with small-scale cleaning, mixing and chopping activities laid out ready for mastery by the young children attending her institute. This represented their initiation into the mysterious ways of grown-ups. Typically in a Montessori nursery children will spend a fair bit of time each day carefully getting out activities from low, child-friendly shelves, laying them out on the floor, doing each of the activities in a structured way, and putting them away again. Perhaps they will sniff little wooden containers to match scents in pairs. Maybe next they will stack pink cubes carefully in order, building a big tower. Later, they might polish a miniature brass teapot with a tiny cloth. Meanwhile, the nursery staff will observe which activities the child is choosing, keep a careful record to ensure they are engaging with a broad range of activities, and gently guide the child through the learning process with a characteristically light touch. As Maria Montessori said, 'Play is children's work'.

Montessori cylinders (Source: Wikimedia Commons) – these are shown carefully ordered and stacked in an approved manner that corresponds with the intention of the Montessori programme

Despite significant attempts to relate to our young, we don't always appreciate fully how children are seeing the world at any particular time, even though most of us try very hard to do so. Our problems probably lie in the fact that we take the concept of childhood for granted. After all, we've all been children at one time or another, so it's something that seems normal and natural to us. We even make the assumption that everyone else shares our idea of what it means to be a child.

The research paints a different picture, however. What if we were to suggest that there may be as many views of childhood as there are people? Admittedly some of these views might overlap, but the whole definition is fraught with confusion and contradiction. In this chapter we will explain several different ways of looking at childhood, as a concept, that we have come across during the course of our research. This will hopefully give you a sense of how difficult it is for politicians, businesses and the like to pin down exactly what we all mean by 'childhood' when they are trying to come up with sensible policies and products to benefit society.

Defining childhood

Any talk of childhood in national and international political policy documents is usually twinned with some sort of statement about 'youth being the future', as though adults represent the past. There is also a lot of worry about what it means to be a child, and how children fit into society generally. UNESCO made the first major attempt to stimulate discussion and policy development on the world stage in 1979 with its International Year of the Child. This was a development of the Declaration of the Rights of the Child from 1924 and later revised in 1959. It triggered a major debate on the subject, including a surprising theory that the whole idea of childhood was a recent invention and that historically it simply hadn't existed as an entity in its own right.[1]

If we look at the matter forensically, we find there are four different categories of childhood that are possible, each varying in the way childhood is seen philosophically, and in its relationship with society as a whole. The four categories are childhood as a biological phenomenon, childhood as a developmental process, childhood as a moral state and childhood as a consumerist opportunity.

Looking at childhood this way provides a useful way of framing different viewpoints, so we will explore them in more detail in the next section. This will also act as an introduction to the book as a whole.

Childhood as a biological phenomenon

Even though we might see childhood as a biological process of some kind, our view of how this plays out in real life reflects our particular vantage point as adults. Invariably children are frequently seen as physically smaller and weaker than adults. Children are seen as needing coddling in some way, and protecting from harm. If you have ever turned on the television during the day and seen advertisements aimed at anxious parents at home looking after young children, you will have seen that they are often for things like branded kitchen disinfectant or special kinds of nappies and creams that are supposed to protect little

---

1   These theories have been hotly debated. See the archived Radio 4 series *The Invention of Childhood* presented by Michael Morpurgo, with related book by Hugh Cunningham (2006).

bottoms more than their commercial rivals. These advertisements are manipulating the natural inclination of parents to have an enhanced concern for the biological aspects of childhood. More seriously, an emphasis on protecting children as vulnerable beings also underpins many other late 20th and early 21st century social trends. For example, it goes some way towards explaining the arguments of some anti-vaccination groups. In fact, vaccination is a particularly interesting case study of biological childhood (as perceived by parents) coming into direct conflict with government policy and the desire to serve and/or control a population, so we will take a moment to discuss it here. It also tells us a great deal about how the human body always exists within a wider social context.

The anti-vaccination movement is nothing new. There have been arguments against vaccination (rapidly made compulsory by government) since the time of Edward Jenner and the introduction of the smallpox vaccine. In England in the 19th century, this was a citizens' protest movement loosely linked to demands for the extension of the vote to ordinary working men, the women's suffrage movement, and resistance to outrages such as women being legally required to submit to spot checks for venereal disease (thanks to the UK's Contagious Diseases Acts of the 1860s).[2] By the 1880s, the protest movement was in full force, with the city of Leicester being at the centre. A local paper at the time reported an impressive anti-vaccination march that took place in March 1885 of around 20,000 protestors accompanied by a brass band, and carrying banners, an effigy of Jenner, and a child's coffin. By 1898 the UK's Vaccination Act meant that parents were allowed to be 'conscientious objectors' and their children could be exempt from vaccination programmes without their parents being fined or sent to prison for non-compliance. Around that time, smallpox outbreaks in the United States led to increased compulsory vaccination there, and alongside this, associated protests. In both the US and the UK, the idea that the state could tell people to put something perceived as potentially harmful into children's bodies caused

---

2   See Nadja Durbach's painstakingly researched book *Bodily matters: The anti-vaccination movement in England, 1853–1907* (London, Duke University Press) for an extensive account of the movement.

considerable concern, even though statistically it could be seen quite easily that the practice led to reduced fatality rates. The problem was that these statistics represented population-level information apparently remote from the family situation. On the other hand, parents looking at individual children quite naturally felt an overwhelming desire to protect their offspring from any immediate harm, their anxieties compounded by the thought of putting something alien into their children physically. Hence they felt compelled to resist, especially when it was the hand of the state intervening into private family life.

Over the next century there was to be periodic concern as to whether vaccination led to neurological damage, and at various stages different vaccines were reviewed and assessed to establish whether this was the case, particularly in the light of the Andrew Wakefield measles, mumps and rubella (MMR) vaccine controversy of 1998.[3] Publicly available vaccines have been found to be extremely low risk, but the function of this chapter is not to review the data, present a case, and take sides in the debate (so please don't write in to lobby us). It is to highlight the way childhood can be seen as a biological state, with children seen as needing protection, in this case from the hand of the state (or micro-organisms as in TV advertisements, or latterly perhaps, the pharmaceutical industry). This is in the face of statistical data that indicate conclusively a child is statistically less likely to die or to suffer neurological damage if you have him or her vaccinated, plus they are less likely to pass a potentially fatal disease on to others. Strictly scientific logic does not always prevail when parents are worried about their own children being potentially harmed on their watch, a matter we will come back to again and again throughout the book, but most significantly in chapter 2, which asks how risky it is to be a child.

In chapter 4, we look at another aspect of biological childhood where we discuss issues such as websex and sexting. We chose these topics because

---

3   Wakefield, A. J. et al. (1998) 'Ileal-lymphoid-nodular hyperplasia, non-specific colitis, and pervasive developmental disorder in children.' *The Lancet*, 351(9103) 28 February: pp. 637-641. This paper is now formally retracted, and an explanation why can be found here: www.bmj.com/content/342/bmj.c7452.full.print

we wanted to explain some of the ways that adolescence muddies the water of what we think of as childhood, once it gets involved with sex. We also take a special look at the social media platforms that enable children to participate in this kind of online activity, and we explore how far this is purely developmental as opposed to rooted in bullying. Our position on this is that there are times a parent needs to be worried about sex and the internet, but it is not a foregone conclusion that your offspring are in the process of being wholly corrupted just because the matter has appeared on the family or school radar. Any panic may in fact be unwarranted, and you might be amazed how genuinely thoughtful your children may be, as we have seen again and again in our research focus groups with teenagers. We have concluded that it is the quality of the conversation you are able to have with your children which will determine whether any damage is taking place. Sticking adult heads in the sand over such matters, or engaging in authoritarian control tactics, are both approaches that serve young people badly. Instead, young people tell us that parents need to have intelligent debates with their children about the role of technology in their lives. We have been warned.

Childhood as a developmental process

In this understanding of childhood, the idea that childhood is an evolutionary state is key. It is widely known that children gradually display behaviours that have helped humans as a species to survive, such as walking and speech, and that these usually appear in a fairly predictable order, known as Gesell's Maturational Theory, from the work of Arnold Gesell (1880-1961) at the Yale Clinic of Child Development, during the first half of the 20th century.[4] More recently, the importance of a particular time frame for child development has been explored, first by psychologists such as Jean Piaget (1896-1980)[5], and then in the work

---

4   See Gesell, A. (1927) 'The measurement and prediction of mental growth.' *Psychological Review*, 34(5) Sep: pp. 385-390 and Gesell, A. (1929) 'Maturation and infant behaviour pattern.' *Psychological Review*, 36(4) Jul: pp. 307-319.

5   Jean Piaget was a prolific author, but see Piaget, J. and Inhelder, B. (1958) *The growth of logical thinking from childhood to adolescence.* New York: Basic Books.

of developmental psychologist Urie Bronfenbrenner (1917-2005), who labelled this phenomenon 'ecological systems theory'. Bronfenbrenner saw the development of the child as being located within the social world, both at the level of the home[6] and also within the wider environment. His work went a long way to influencing the provision of rehabilitative education for disabled children in particular.

For the purposes of this book, therefore, the 'developmental process' category focuses on childhood as a kind of 'work in progress', along the lines of Sandra pottering about with her wheelbarrow. Children are busy engaged in the process of growing up, either because someone has set out a series of activities aimed at helping them to do this (the writings of classic education authors such as Locke, Rousseau, Piaget, Montessori and Fröbel deal with this quite extensively) or simply because the child has decided to initiate the process for him or herself. Right in the middle of this version of childhood we see a debate about whether children are effectively a 'blank slate' upon which learning could be written (as described by the philosopher John Locke in 1690[7]), or 'natural beings' who needed civilising (as Jean-Jacques Rousseau put it in 1762[8]). It's probably a mixture of both (Steven Pinker explained an evolutionary basis for this in terms of psychology in 2002[9]) with children looking around them for tacit instructions on how to grow into adults, while also learning the codes of conduct expected of them in different societies. The 19th century educationalist G. Stanley Hall described this psychological struggle of children between the known and the not-yet-known very well in one of his early books in 1893:

'...the linguistic imperfections of children are far more often shown in combining words than in naming the concrete things they know

6   For an overview of some of this research, see Bronfenbrenner, U. (1986) 'Ecology of the family as a context for human development: Research perspectives.' *Developmental Psychology*, 22(6): pp. 723-742.

7   See Locke, J. (1689) *An essay concerning human understanding*, Book II, Chapter 1, 2.

8   See Rousseau, J. J. (1762) *Emile, or on education*. Translated by A. Bloom. New York: Basic Books (1979).

9   See Pinker, S. (2002) *The blank slate: The modern denial of human nature*. Harmondsworth: Penguin.

*or do not know. To name an object is a passion with them, for it is
to put their own mark upon it, to appropriate it.*[10]

Stanley Hall's explanation reminds us of Conrad, one of Sandra's
children at the age of two, who spent some time in the back garden
looking in amazement at a hot-air balloon in the sky while trying to
work out what the new, marvellous object was. 'SKY!' he said, pointing.
Then 'SKYBALL!' he announced. Then suddenly noticing that there was
a little basket with people in underneath it, the item was re-described.
'SKYBALLCAR!' Satisfied, Conrad looked to nearby adults for approval.
To his mind, and admittedly to theirs as well, he had described the hot-
air balloon perfectly.

Incidentally, while praise when children make an effort to speak and
label things is important, research tells us that, for most children,
more input or correction from parents doesn't necessarily mean better
progress. Researchers invariably find that it is a question of finding
a sensible middle ground with parents, or teachers, being interested
enough in what's going on, and imparting enough information, leaving
enough space for children to experiment for themselves to good effect.
In this way, perfectly good terminology developed by children enters the
family vernacular. We all have words and phrases unique to our own
families that have come about in this way, and we should enjoy them. The
correct terms can find their way in gently as time goes on.

Loosely linked to this developmental concept of childhood, in chapter 2
we talk about risk, and in chapter 6 we look at how biometrics are used
in schools to measure and track children as they go through their daily
routines. Both of these issues are interesting to explore because they tell
us a great deal about where children's development comes into conflict
with the desire of wider society to control them. This has the effect of
removing some of their developmental opportunities as their social (and
sometimes geographical) space for exploration and experimentation
effectively shrinks.

---

10   Stanley Hall, G. (1893) *The contents of children's minds on entering
      school.* New York and Chicago: E. L. Kellogg & co. p. 32.

Childhood as a moral state

The epicentre of state control is the application of law, but how it relates to children depends on where they live. This is because the age of criminal responsibility varies in different countries, ranging from eight in Scotland to 12 in the Netherlands and Canada. Before this age, children are not seen as being able to take legal responsibility for their own actions, and are therefore deemed innocent of consequences. We often see young children as being innocent in this way, a position that is often rooted in religious doctrine (you only have to think of the *putti* baby angels, apparently devoid of original sin, adorning Raphael's Sistine Madonna, to see this mentality at work).

For a darker view, however, it's worth taking a look at the 1955 book *Lolita* by Vladimir Nabokov with its controversial handling of paedophilia and sexualised childhood, quite remote from the contemporary awareness of harm such practices can cause. There we have an altogether different kind of moral mindset in relation to childhood, one which displays a child as sexually active, and in doing so shows scant regard for the moral rights of children.[11] This is not a position many people would feel at all comfortable with.

It's easy to be outraged about child abuse, as it strikes at the heart of what it means to be a child within our society, as well as an adult. Previous generations focused on violent 'baby battering' in a similar way, and it is important we care about all of these things if we are to meet our obligations properly in raising the next generation. Yet if we are to respect children properly, it follows that we must also pay attention to less obvious ways of harming them that take place. Their digital privacy rights are a larger part of this than we might realise. All too often children are seen as subservient to the demands of the state

---

11   For example 'Lolita, light of my life, fire of my loins. My sin, my soul. Lo-lee-ta: the tip of the tongue taking a trip of three steps down the palate to tap, at three, on the teeth. Lo. Lee. Ta. She was Lo, plain Lo, in the morning, standing four feet ten in one sock. She was Lola in slacks. She was Dolly at school. She was Dolores on the dotted line. But in my arms she was always Lolita.' From Nabokov, V. (1955) *Lolita*. Paris: Olympia Press, Ch 1.

when it comes to schooling, welfare support and healthcare. Since the growth of the personal computer, and associated database packages, they have increasingly been audited and tracked minutely across digital systems, whether they like it or not, and any number of grounds are invoked for this, most usually something to do with safeguarding their wellbeing along the lines of 'you can't be too careful'. Oddly enough, we are finding in our research that excessive tracking is leading to a form of hyperconnected childhood in which there is no escape from scrutiny, contributing to new anxieties about children's lives and happiness. We discuss this important development in more detail in chapter 5.

Childhood as a consumerist opportunity

Children and their parents are often marketed to intensively before birth. In the UK, the Bounty Pack offered to mothers at their first antenatal appointment or on the postnatal ward in hospitals contains several little cards containing requests for names, addresses and expected dates of delivery, with marketeers keen to invite parents to buy their products or invest in their financial packages. The mothers-to-be are reeled in with the promise of try-before-you-buy samples of goods such as sensitive washing powder, nappy cream and premium disposable nappies. Recipients of the packs (which is almost every mother in the UK) may later find their personal data has been sold to other private companies, who are also keen to target young families (although technically they can opt out from this). The families portrayed in the packs may these days be racially diverse, but they all fit into a bright, shiny aspirational model of family life which relies on commercially produced and heavily marketed and branded goods in order to stay afloat.

This marketing offensive continues as the child grows. If you want to understand how consumerism impacts on everyday life for children, just walk into a large chain toyshop. With dolls dressed in pink and construction sets packaged in blue, it's clear to even the youngest children where the gender divide lies in terms of cultural expectations of them. Many academics and social commentators who grew up in households that embraced unisex dungarees and gender-neutral Lego in the late 1960s to early 1980s are particularly sensitised to this type of change, and they have described this process – with some professional horror –

as 'pinkification'. In this way toys both reflect and exaggerate different social divisions within society. It is the same in many large clothing stores, with a solitary row of grungy sports-style clothes aimed at young boys acting as a foil to the half dozen or so rows of massively varied and colourful outfits aimed at little girls. The subliminal message here is that boys play outside and need robust clothing to withstand the onslaught of everyday life, whereas girls need to think more about looking nice and varying their outfits. What happens as a consequence of this kind of commercial practice is that a heavily marketised model of childhood gradually replaces the real thing, which a lot of authors and thinkers have argued is having the effect of disempowering children and removing some of their choices in life. The pressure for parents – and children – to respond to consumerism and spend is also having harmful effects on children's wider engagement with society, with children increasingly being defined in terms of their family's consumption. Home-knitted sweaters are apparently out; glittery nail polish is apparently in.

Children in the digital age

We have carefully unpicked four different models of childhood, so it's possible to see how views vary, and where some of the main fault lines might be. It's clear even the word 'childhood' means many different things to different people. This is no doubt why policies dealing with children can end up appearing to look so confused. Yet one thing stands out for us, and that is that we think the most difficult area for children, and the most fragile fault line, is between children and consumerism. It certainly dominates public debate frequently enough. Increased disposable income combined with the mass production of consumer goods has led to something of a social free-for-all in which children have to try to find an identity in a complex world with vested interests – that can be very confusing. For example, we saw a beautiful wooden garden playhouse aimed at children up to the age of 11 recently, which was being marketed at junior-aged girls so they could escape out of the house with their tablet computers. This is in stark contrast to the previously perceived function of a playhouse, to allow young children to 'play house' with tea sets and miniature brooms and so on. The new function, involving trading contact with people in the family home for isolated engagement with an online environment, seems to be emblematic of the mixed messages many children receive about their role in society, as well as the developmental options open to them. Would we feel the same if the girls were being encouraged to escape into the playhouse with a book? Probably not, because we are academics and by definition somewhat bookish ourselves. But we could justify this by saying that a book encourages a rich internal life and dialogue that sets children up for a world of intellectual adventure, whereas interacting with a tablet computer runs the risk of encouraging inattention and passive entertainment consumption in its place. Therefore, it's a complicated problem, and one that demands conscious reflection from adults (in other words, encourage balance in children's lives rather than letting them spend too much time focusing on just one activity, even if it is *Minecraft* and they are attempting to build an entire virtual model of Mount Olympus with their friends, as one of Sandra's children did recently).

Schooling and childhood

While most of children's lives will be spent at home with their families, a significant proportion is spent at school in most cases. We see conflicting classifications of childhood causing difficulties here as well. One example of troubled classification is the gendered presence of school uniforms and their overtones of medieval sumptuary laws (controlling who was allowed to wear certain things at certain times depending on their status or rank, which now manifests itself in rules like boys not being allowed to wear skirts and girls not being allowed to wear trousers). Other examples of classification conflict include complaints that children are turning up to start school with poorly developed speech (regardless of the actual age of children and whether English is their first language), confusion as to whether UK school pupils over the age of 18 require police checks in order to participate in certain residential activities (they don't), and careers organisations selling university applicant data to third parties for profit regardless of data protection laws. In all of these, the social identity of the child or young person is complex and reflects the priorities and concerns of adults around him or her, but it doesn't always sit very comfortably.

This carries over into education management systems. In the modern world, children are mere data points on large-scale interconnected landscapes of measurement. Do they have free school meals (a UK measure of deprivation)? What is their native tongue? Do they have any special educational needs? What is their address? Have they broken any rules lately? Their identities are broken down into fragmented models from which policymakers try to derive meaning, with a view to improving the system or attracting additional funding. In this way, childhood becomes a kind of commodity with which education systems can trade. The more affluent the background of the pupil, the higher status they are to the school, as statistically the school's path to a good external inspection or good examination results becomes easier. Deprived pupils, on the other hand, are sometimes seen in policy documents as having defective childhoods in some way (what sociologists might call uncharitably a 'spoiled identity' in technical terms), allegedly making life harder for their teachers. Yet deprived pupils frequently attract a higher level of financial resource from government. Schools in countries where choice exists therefore have a balancing act ahead of them. They need to position themselves in marketing terms according to the position where they feel they can maximise outputs and gain most respect, even if it sometimes means focusing on a subset of the local community at the expense of fringe cases. So here we see that, even in a system explicitly set up to cater for the needs of children, childhood identities are confused and blurred by a range of adult concerns as institutions navigate a complicated social path.

In this way childhood is always changing, as the adults around it change. The digital revolution has played a significant role here. Children find themselves in a new social space where existing identities brush up against new ones, where old forms of danger and discrimination sit side by side with revelatory concerns as new technologies emerge. We need to explore how this is happening if we want to create wholesome and rewarding childhoods for 21st century children. The next chapter starts this process, by taking an overview of risk in the lives of children, and giving a steer as to how worried we should be (hint: not very).

Chapter 2
How risky is it to be a child?

Sometimes it seems as though it's a jungle out there. We are perpetually bombarded with news images and reports of children coming to harm, and just when we think we have recovered, they report some more. The problem is that we are hard-wired to react to images of children in distress. If we weren't, then there probably wouldn't be a human race any longer.

One of the most iconic children-in-danger images of all time is that of Kim Phuc, as a nine-year-old girl running from a napalm attack in the Vietnam War on 8 June 1972. No doubt you will know the photo, which probably more than anything else, contributed to the ending of the conflict. The picture, taken by 21-year-old press photographer Nick Ut, shows us children screaming in horror, with one badly burned and naked, having torn off her clothes in pain after the chemical attack. The children are surrounded by soldiers and you can't see what they are running from. The picture covered the front pages of all the newspapers at the time, its news value overriding the obvious nudity in the photo, which would normally have been a problem for many international news organisations.

In terms of social impact, the contemporary equivalent of the Kim Phuc picture is that of Alan Kurdi, a three-year-old Syrian child washed up on Bodrum beach in Turkey on 2 September 2015, as his family tried to flee the conflict and escape to join relatives in Canada. Once again, we see a picture that presses a lot of psychological buttons for us, in this case a vulnerable child barely out of toddlerhood lying face down on a beach, almost as though he is asleep, waves washing backwards and forwards over him, and an official looking on, before retrieving the boy.

It is human nature to want to protect small children, and we never want to see them in a position such as this. However, one thing that human nature is not very good at, is assessing the overall risk of really bad things happening to children.

The Oxford University economist Max Roser is part of the Our World in Data team, which uses empirical statistical data to assess global development over time. In an extensive and very detailed discussion of child mortality data from around the middle of the 18th century to the present day, Max states the root of the perception problem very clearly. 'One reason why we do not see progress,' he says, 'is that we are unaware of how bad the past was.' The reverse of this applies as well, of course, in that we often think things are more dangerous for modern children than they actually are. The reason for this misconception is that the concept of risk is socially constructed and relates to things such as where we are in history, the political environment around us, and what we are used to seeing happen where we live. If we have access to 24-hour rolling news and it is full of stories of death and disaster, our pre-industrial era brains engage in something that psychologists would call 'confirmation bias', a situation in which we look out for the information that supports our existing beliefs. If we have already decided the world is a dangerous place, then it is harder to persuade us to look at conflicting data that might change the way we think.

It's the job of academics to encourage people to do this, however, so let's borrow some of Max Roser's analysis on child mortality to start things off. Max makes the point that dramatic things have happened in terms of reductions in child mortality, but they happen so slowly this is of little interest to news organisations. We don't have full datasets for all of these countries (the UK data is only from 1922 onwards, for example) but they are representative of the fact that child mortality of under-fives has plummeted since the mid-18th century. Statistically speaking, things are definitely safer, to the tune of something like 455 fewer young children dying each day.

Most parents in the developed world today will be aware that their families are likely to be smaller, and thanks to vaccinations and antibiotics, as well as smaller family size, their children's health is likely to be pretty good. It is children in low-income economies who really have it tough, as they face war, famine, illness, infectious disease and vulnerability to a range of natural disasters including earthquakes, mudslides and tsunamis. Given that we know all this, why are anxious headlines in newspapers about children so prevalent? The answer is something called 'moral panic', something we'll discuss in some detail now, as it needs to be understood if we are to appreciate the reasoning behind many of our decisions on children's upbringing and education.

What is moral panic?

You know that creeping sensation that things are not quite right, and the world is changing about you in ways you can't quite put into words? The feeling that society is turning on its axis in a bad way, and things have just got a lot more threatening? The sense that the media is full of stories about disasters around every corner? That's moral panic, and it takes a surprising amount of work for an individual to override. The term was first used in relation to children and society by the author Stanley Cohen in his 1972 book *Folk Devils and Moral Panics*, which explored the relationship between young people and the media (in this case showing how Mods and Rockers were portrayed as being outside the mainstream and therefore in some way dangerous). The term may be relatively new, but the concept of folk devils and moral panic is a lot older. We'll list a few of the more digitally-related ones here, and try to establish why they are worrying, as well as gauging their likely risk to children and young people.

Witchcraft

Witchcraft represented one of the first examples of moral panic, so it is useful to track its path through its early history, not least because it is experiencing growing digital interest among teens at present. It has complex origins, but arguably reached its apotheosis in Great Britain with Parliament's *Act against Conjuration, Witchcraft and dealing with evil and wicked spirits* (1604). This Act paved the way for the self-anointed 'Witchfinder General' Matthew Hopkins to roam East Anglia during a brief but infamous period in the 1640s, torturing and executing as many as 300 women in the pursuit of status and personal profit (and no men). Along with the US Salem witchcraft trials and execution of 20 people in the 1690s, we normally associate such

31

anxiety with the somewhat febrile spiritual atmosphere of the 17th century, a period in which the Reformation and Puritanism both came to the fore. This particular folk devil and moral panic lasted beyond Hopkins' reign of terror, however. As Young explains,[12] people were still being accused of witchcraft in the Cambridgeshire Fens as late as the 1930s, suggesting it has something of an enduring quality. Even now, it also occasionally features in Reuters news reports from places like Tanzania, Congo, India and the Central African Republic, where attacks on alleged witches are often linked to regional political power struggles.

Yet in the UK by the 1950s witchcraft had more or less faded from public consciousness, being replaced by a focus on spiritual practice such as Wicca, in which there is concern for the environment, the rhythm of the year, and fertility, among other things. (Wicca should not be seen as interchangeable with witchcraft, nor related to Satanic Ritual Abuse, a popular moral panic of the 1980s-1990s.) This has led to a situation today where it is possible for young teenagers to follow openly the hashtag #witchesofinstagram on social media, post up pictures of their tastefully arranged home altars on the social media site Pinterest, and buy boxes of attractive pagan accoutrements through the post via a monthly subscription service. This new, public, teen-friendly face of witchcraft may lead us to think that the associated moral panic has passed, but we would be mistaken, particularly given the frequency of associated international news reports.

Mindful of this, social anthropology lecturers have a way of demonstrating to young people how we are all prone to being pulled into the same 'othering' mindset through a game they sometimes play in lectures. 'Let's pretend someone in this room is a witch,' they say to their undergraduates. 'I am not going to say who the witch is, but I want you to think very carefully and then write the person's name on a piece of paper, that we will then collect up.' Frighteningly often, there is one dominant name that comes out of the mix, and that person will usually be female and have some distinguishing characteristic that makes her more identifiable from the rest of the group, perhaps as a consequence

---

12   Young, F. (2013) *Witches and witchcraft in Ely: A history*. Ely: independently published.

of informal racial profiling, demeanour or appearance. This way we can see that this particular folk devil continues to bubble away just below the surface of society, and it has never really disappeared. It may take different forms, for example prejudice or some sort of tacit profiling of people who are thought to cause problems, but the principle is the same – some people are seen as being on the outside of the dominant group, and are less than welcome because of it. Therefore, witchcraft can take two forms. It can be classified as subversive by groups seeking a dominant status within an unsettled society, while at the same time being classified as little more than a benign consumer lifestyle in more stable societies.

If we are going to assess the risk of witchcraft to children and young people, the main problem here is the isolated nature of a quasi-religious practice that is largely encouraged by social media. This is very different from a real-life community centred around religious practice and made up of different, inter-dependent demographic groups in which the young person can find diverse role models among those at different life stages. There is also the potential for children and young people to make unfavourable physical comparisons with idealised images of witches on social media, which may contribute to anxiety about their physical appearance. Both are relatively minor risks and as long as young people have a variety of solid relationships in their lives, then a transient dose of online witchcraft is unlikely to do any harm, and it may even make them think more carefully about important things like the planet and climate change, willing other people well through acts of loving kindness, and pausing for thought and reflection during a busy teenage week.

Video games
Luckily for us in Great Britain we don't have a Witchfinder General any longer, but we do have alternative bogeymen to occupy our minds. Areas that the media tends to link closely to the lives of children and young people include video games. There seems to have been calls for regulation for almost as long as graphic videos have been in existence. When you think about it, any parent seeing their child spending long hours in sepulchral gloom shooting at avatars in a shower of blood and guts is quite naturally going to be concerned about the impact this activity might have on their son or daughter's wellbeing. Associated with that is

the concern that children will become somehow brutalised or otherwise inured to violence (this represents the model of childhood as innocence, if you recall from the previous chapter). There is also significant concern about the amount of time young people spend online playing games, and whether this is likely to affect their mental health, social development and their educational development.

Many researchers have explored these questions. Mindful of societal concerns, in 2015 the Task Force on Violent Media of the American Psychological Association (APA) carried out a review of all the research into whether video games promote violence, published as the *Technical Report on the Review of the Violent Video Game Literature.*[13] At the time, there was substantial criticism of the APA study on the grounds that some of the literature included hadn't been subject to peer review (i.e. subject to the gold standard of quality control by fellow scientists and academics), culminating in an open letter signed by 230 leading researchers in the field objecting to the findings. The report argued that there was a link between violent computer games and aggression, although they admitted there was limited research into use by younger children, and effects over time, as well as the fact that the problem was a complex one and involved various risk factors not easily or readily described in the mass media. Subsequently other critics have pointed out that effects vary among young people playing identical games in different countries, suggesting a correlation rather than causation – in other words, we can't be sure of whether aggressive young people tend to play more video games, or whether video games make them aggressive (and many have argued it is likely to be the former).

Researchers have also tried to establish what the impact of regular online gaming might be in other respects, and this is less controversial. In 2014 Isabela Granic, Adam Lobel and Rutger Engels of Radboud University in the Netherlands published a thoughtful review on the educational and social benefits of video games, under the title *The Benefits of*

---

13   APA task force on violent media. (2015) *Technical report on the review of the violent video game literature*. Available at: www.apa.org/pi/families/review-video-games.pdf (Accessed: 6 August 2021).

Playing Video Games in the leading American Psychological Association academic journal *American Psychologist*. What is interesting about this article, which is readily available in PDF form and particularly accessible to the lay reader,[14] is the authors' obvious understanding of the role of games in the lives of adolescents and young people, as well as their rich understanding of the different genres and nuances of games. They map them out on a diagram ranging from simple to complex on one axis, and social to non-social on the other. Then they plot them so it's possible to get a sense of the wider gaming landscape and what the likely impact of different games might be. This way, it's possible to see that complex multi-player games are likely to have a completely different place in the online worlds of young people than, say, solo shoot-'em-ups experienced in isolation. As young people negotiate multi-layered virtual worlds with their friends, the authors argue that they become increasingly socialised, with co-operative behaviour largely rewarded. Creativity is also thought to be enhanced. There are many other studies coming to similar conclusions, which act as a counterpoint to the American Psychological Association task force report. Clearly there are advantages and disadvantages to gaming, so how do we best support young people as they embark on their online experiences?

We know from our own research with children and young people that while kids are gaming, it's not unusual for two things to be going on at once – engaging in massive online play with others, via a platform such as Steam, while at the same time chatting away in the corner of the screen to friends about what is set for homework or which PE kit they need to take in that week to school. The authors of the academic article under discussion conclude that the engaging, pro-social aspects of gaming even offer possibilities for improving mental health. We don't know how much impact something like this is likely to have yet, but what we do know is that, far from being overwhelmingly negative, many games are seen as works of art in their own right.

It's for this reason that organisations such as the British Academy of Film and Television Art (BAFTA) offer sector-specific games awards

---

14   APA. (2013) *The benefits of playing video games.* Available at: www.apa. org/pubs/journals/releases/amp-a0034857.pdf (Accessed: 6 August 2021).

and support young games designers. They are seen in the same light as film and TV in terms of artistic classification. Take the example of Sandra's favourite indie game, *Journey*, directed in 2012 by Jenova Chen for PlayStation 3 and 4, and published by thatgamecompany, with music by Austin Wintory. There is a clear narrative arc, despite the story being told wordlessly, and players are required to join forces to play with a stranger, whose identity they don't learn until the end of the game. It is designed to invoke feelings of 'smallness and wonder' among players, rather than the usual win/lose mindset. *Journey* won multiple awards, including the BAFTA Games Award for Artistic Achievement in 2013.

The fact that the artistic aspects of video games are being recognised by the industry is important, and we also discuss this at considerable length in chapter 3, in relation to digital ghost stories. When we are trying to decide how children and young people best spend their time, we need to remember the importance of being discriminating about the quality of the content. After all, society has had these debates before. If we look back to a couple of centuries ago, for example, young people (mainly women) were frequently criticised for reading novels, as this was felt to encourage inflamed sexual passions and romanticism, and to be insufficiently intellectual. As it said in 1835 in the article *Devouring Books* in the *American Annals of Education* (p3):

> *'Thousands of young people spend their time in perpetual reading, or rather in devouring books. It is true, the food is light; but it occupies the mental faculties, for the time, in fruitless efforts, and operates to exclude food of a better quality.'*

The quotation doesn't sound all that different from criticisms of gaming in the 21st century. Similarly, if we search the Educational Resources Information Centre (ERIC) database, a leading professional research resource that includes key references to most pre-internet age research papers of significance, we can draw comparisons with anxieties surrounding children and television in the 1970s. During this period, there was significant interest into themes such as the impact of television violence on children, the relationship between television watching and child obesity, possible correlations between television and decreasing literacy among school pupils, and the role television commercials played in children's lives and development. Once again, we can see clear links with the moral panic represented by video games in the current climate. We have obviously been here before (and if we ever get robot babysitters in place, we will probably be here again).

As with many things in the digital world, it is the quality of your conversation with children which will determine whether you are able to divine the risk of harm when they are playing video games. The best way to have a high-quality conversation is to ask them to teach you how to play the games they are interested in (unless you are an expert already, in which case you probably didn't need to read this section).

Stranger danger

Sandra used to be a keen tennis player as a child and when she was nine years old, she attended weekly coaching in a nearby town. On one occasion, her electrical engineer father didn't turn up to collect her from the session as usual. Sandra wasn't too bothered initially, but as she waited she thought this was rather odd as her father tended to be pathologically early for things most of the time. Eventually a car drew up with one of her father's colleagues in it.

'Hello,' he said. 'Your dad has sent me to come to collect you as he has had to take your brother to hospital.'

Sandra thought for a moment. She had been well-briefed in matters pertaining to stranger danger and knew exactly what to say next.

'I've heard about people like you! I can't get in your car because I don't know that's true.'

The driver laughed. 'It is true! But you are quite right to check.' He thought quickly. 'Here's my Electricity Board diary, and if you look, there's my official Electricity Board car radio. So you know I work with your father.'

'I am still not getting into the car,' Sandra replied. They had reached an impasse. Like the rest of her family, Sandra could be very stubborn when it was a matter of principle. It occurred to her that she could even weaponise her junior tennis racquet if necessary.

'I know,' said the driver, 'I will call your dad on the radio and you can talk to him. Blue 21? Blue 21?' The driver summoned her father with his official call sign, which Sandra recognised.

The radio crackled into life. A familiar voice came across the airwaves. 'Blue 21, over.'

'I have your parcel here but it's refusing to be collected. It says it won't get into the car of a stranger, over.'

There was a snort of laughter. 'Sandra, it's your dad here and it's fine, I have sent this man to collect you and you can get in the car. Over.'

Sandra thought for a moment. It sounded authentic. She relented and got into the car. This was fortunate as just then her father was coping with a son who had managed to cut his hand open and a wife who had developed a migraine and couldn't drive him to the accident and emergency department. Sandra was however praised for her self-preservation instinct later that evening.

This incident took place in the summer of 1977, but it is easy to imagine a similar conversation taking place today. It's a parent's worst nightmare, the idea that a child could be abducted and taken into a stranger's car, for the purposes of abuse or murder. Consequently, a lot of effort is put into telling children not to talk to strangers or go off with people they don't know. There are even public information films made about it, for example the *Charley the Cat* series made in 1973, originally created by Richard Taylor Cartoons and voiced by the late Kenny Everett (and later memorably sampled by The Prodigy for their 1991 hit single *Charly*).

What we need to bear in mind when we are thinking about how dangerous it is to be a child is whether the idea of the stranger really represents a statistically significant problem, or whether what is happening is some sort of theoretical conception of danger, which serves another purpose. If we consider the statistics for England, we can see that roughly every 15 years or so, there is an abduction of a young child that results in a homicide. In 2011, there were around 200 attempted abductions of children and teenagers, and about 50 of those were completed (these figures are from the organisation Action Against Abduction). If you were to profile a typical abductee, they would be 11 years old, and female, and asked to get into a car. Therefore, Sandra's danger instincts perhaps had some basis in reality.

However, children are much more likely to die or suffer serious injury in other ways. Each year, around 6000 children die in total in the UK. The statistics of how they die are quite sobering and can be seen in the 2014 report *Why Children Die*, published by the Royal College of Paediatrics and Child Health and the National Children's Bureau. Nearly 2000 children a year die in the UK who, statistically speaking, would not have died if they were born in a country such as Sweden. This is thought to be because of issues such as social inequality leading to differences in healthcare, including variable antenatal care. That doesn't seem to make it to the headlines and there doesn't seem to be a lot of public campaigning about such deaths, apart from the valuable work done by organisations such as SANDS (The Stillbirth and Neonatal Death charity). In addition to this, nearly 500 children die each year through accidents or injury that are often in the home, and many of these deaths are usually preventable. We won't go into the minute details of the comparative statistical risk here, but we have developed a parental anxiety calibration tool which might be helpful in establishing where best to expend our energies in terms of worrying.

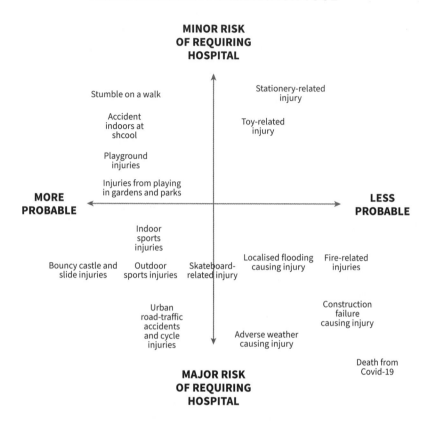

PARENTAL ANXIETY CALIBRATION TOOL

**MINOR RISK
OF REQUIRING
HOSPITAL**

Stumble on a walk

Stationery-related
injury

Accident
indoors at
shcool

Toy-related
injury

Playground
injuries

Injuries from playing
in gardens and parks

**MORE
PROBABLE**

**LESS
PROBABLE**

Indoor
sports
injuries

Localised flooding
causing injury

Fire-related
injuries

Bouncy castle and
slide injuries

Outdoor
sports injuries

Skateboard-
related injury

Urban
road-traffic
accidents
and cycle
injuries

Construction
failure
causing injury

Adverse weather
causing injury

Death from
Covid-19

**MAJOR RISK
OF REQUIRING
HOSPITAL**

In the diagram, we have plotted the relative risk levels to children of different accidents and disasters experienced by children in the UK, which resulted in presentation at a hospital's accident and emergency department. This is based on data from the Royal Society for the Prevention of Accidents (RoSPA) Home and Leisure Accident and Surveillance System, from 1998-2002, which are the most recent years for which we could obtain data. We added the Covid-19 element based on Office for National Statistics data.

Society hasn't changed a great deal since the RoSPA statistics, apart from a couple of factors. The ready availability of back garden trampolines has most likely led to a significant increase in limb injuries and the occasional fatality using them, and this could probably be plotted in the same sector of the grid as bouncy castle and slide injuries. Another change compared to 1998-2002 is that there were no child injuries or deaths relating to terrorism during this period, whereas in 2017 the Manchester Arena bombing led to 18 children under 16 being killed or injured. To put this latter figure into perspective, however, during 2015, 54 children under 16 were killed, 1910 seriously injured and 14,137 slightly injured on roads as car passengers, cyclists and pedestrians in Great Britain (England, Scotland and Wales).[15] These figures look high, but the success story of the 2015 report was how much these figures *had dropped* since 2005. Statistically speaking, things are getting safer for British children (although the roads may simply be safer because children generally go out less; we can't know that from the data as they stand).

Andy undertaking an early risk assessment exercise

---

15   We've derived our data from the government report *Reported road casualties in Great Britain: Main results 2015*. Available at: www.gov.uk/ government/uploads/system/uploads/attachment_data/file/533293/rrcgb-main-results-2015.pdf (Accessed: 6 August 2021).

As Andy's picture shows, things still might not feel that safe out there in the real world, however, so let's think about how different risks compare. Statistically speaking, a British child under 16 had a 0.000100832% chance of being killed or injured in the Manchester bombing (one in a million), and a 0.135292288% chance of being killed or injured on British roads (one in a thousand, which includes many relatively minor injuries that need a couple of stitches or a limb in plaster as result of children falling off bicycles, tripping over their own roller blades and so on). If we look at the abduction data, we can see that there is a 0.000420136% chance of a child being abducted (four in a million, and that includes some children being abducted by people they know, for example a non-resident parent). Two of these risks are so tiny that in purely rational terms, it's not worth spending a disproportionate amount of time worrying about them, and one is significantly higher and needs greater attention, namely the risk of road traffic accidents. After all, for every child abduction victim, there are 250 children who are killed or injured on British roads. Why are we not worrying about road safety 250 times as much? Why aren't there 250 times as many stories on road safety in British newspapers than there are about child abductees? (The same applies to the risk of children dying from Covid-19, where the risk is also one in a million, according to the Office for National Statistics, and so far confined to children with very serious pre-existing conditions where they might not have survived anyway.)

The answer is that incidences of terrorist attack and child abduction are so vanishingly rare that they are of particular interest to the media, and to society in its current news-hungry state. Here lies the root of moral panic, which is how we started this chapter. That's because risk is fluid as a concept, as many sociologists have explained. The leading authority Ulrich Beck writes:

> 'Risk is not synonymous with catastrophe. Risk means the anticipation of catastrophe. Risks concern the possibility of future occurrences and developments; they make present a state of the world that does not (yet) exist. Whereas every catastrophe is spatially, temporally and socially determined, the anticipation of catastrophe lacks any spatio-temporal or social concreteness.'[16]

---

16   Beck, U. (2007) *World at risk*. Cambridge: Polity Press. p. 9.

The problem with stranger danger is therefore that it is a vague risk. Sometimes children report that people in cars try to stop to speak to them, but more often than not it's an innocent request for directions or information. However, by the time this has been established, anxieties have proliferated, thanks to schools sending out danger warnings to parent email lists, and also announcing in form time and assembly that children need to be extra vigilant. Consequently, children become fearful that being snatched on their way home from school by someone that they don't know is more likely than it is in reality. This is further fuelled by news reports of potential abductions, for example, the 2016 example of a young girl in Oxfordshire who was found knocking on people's doors asking for help, when it was later discovered from CCTV footage that no abduction could have taken place. Historic abuse allegations become conflated with the idea of stranger danger, adding to the general culture of fear. These include multiple historic reports of children being abused by people they should be able to trust, such as the staff of the Haut de la Garenne children's home in Jersey, members of religious organisations, such as monks at Buckfast Abbey School, hospital doctors such as the children's cancer specialist Myles Bradbury at Addenbrooke's Hospital in Cambridge, and television celebrities involved with children's charities such as Jimmy Savile and Rolf Harris. The very immediacy and extent of social media and mass media reporting combine to make it very difficult for children and their parents to scale anxiety. Nowhere and nobody seems safe.

It all seems very disorientating and a very far cry from the free and easy, sunlit world of the 1930s where children went off to play on their own for hours at a time. German psychologist Martha Muchow spent a great deal of time in Hamburg between the two World Wars, minutely tracking the geography of how and where children played. Parks and streets became improvised playgrounds as children spent a great deal of time in small groups without adults, and Muchow's classic and highly regarded study *The Life Space of the Urban Child*[17] is filled with maps depicting quite large areas

---

17   Muchow, M., & Muchow, H. H. (2015) 'The life space of the urban child – The loss and discovery, connections and requisites'. In Mey, G., and Günther, H. (eds.) *The life space of the urban child: Perspectives on Martha Muchow's classic study.* New Brunswick, NJ: Transaction Publishers, pp. 63–146. (original work published 1935).

within which children were more or less free to roam. Muchow's research is usually invoked when academics are considering how play habits have changed across generations, along with how far children are allowed to stray. The general consensus is that over the last four generations, roaming areas have shrunk substantially and it is now quite rare for children to be out without adults in the UK, even if they are walking to school with other children. The irony of this situation is that the fewer children seen out on the streets alone, the less adults expect to see them there, potentially making it more dangerous for children. This is because drivers are not looking out for them, and environments are not planned with small pedestrians in mind. The contrast with countries such as Finland or the Netherlands is marked. There, even five-year-olds are allowed to hop on their bikes and whizz up to see Grandma around the corner without having to take an adult along with them for safety. When children have the freedom to move about, this brings with it the freedom to engage in regular daily exercise, which brings us to another moral panic – child obesity.

Obesity

With column inches to fill, food always makes a good story. Whether it's food miles, seasonal food, supermarket waste, underpaid farmers or food scares, newspapers and websites use this as a method of engaging with their readers at a most intimate level. We are probably all familiar with the rhetoric here. A culture of processed food and sedentary living means that more of us are overweight than ever before. The most obese are the poorest among us.

Historically speaking, this state of affairs is unusual, and we'll begin with a look at the phenomenon of school feeding to explain why. By school feeding, we mean making provision for children to be given meals during the school day, something that started in 1906 under a Liberal government with the Education (Provision of Meals) Act, after there were widespread concerns regarding many children being underweight and growth rates being relatively poor. Various experiments took place, for example in 1907 in Bradford, where Jonathan Priestley (father of the author J B Priestley), was headmaster of the Green Lane School and involved in the initiative. As part of the experiment, children's weight gain was carefully tracked, as can be seen in the chart below.

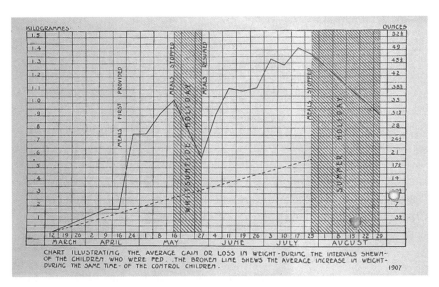

CHART ILLUSTRATING THE AVERAGE GAIN OR LOSS IN WEIGHT-DURING THE INTERVALS SHEWN- OF THE CHILDREN WHO WERE FED. ,THE BROKEN LINE SHEWS THE AVERAGE INCREASE IN WEIGHT- DURING THE SAME TIME- OF THE CONTROL CHILDREN .   1907

Source: National Archives

A dinner lady who was part of the Bradford Education Committee's initiative described the progress of one experiment as follows:

'Breakfast consisted every day of oatmeal porridge with milk and treacle, followed by bread and margarine or dripping, with milk, hot or cold, to drink ... It will be noticed that oatmeal porridge was given to the children every day. I ascertained from the children that only one of them was in the habit of eating porridge, and he was a Scotch child. At the first breakfast 13 of them refused to eat it; the next day there were only 2, and from that day it was eaten and enjoyed by all. It was originally intended to have varied the diet for breakfast but on any occasion when this was done the children were so disappointed at having no porridge, that practically no alteration in the menu was made. A more satisfactory breakfast, from the food value point of view probably cannot be given for the money. (Miss Cuff, Dinner Lady)'[18]

---

18 Extract and graph taken from City of Bradford Education Committee
    Report by the Medical Superintendent, Ralph H Crowley MD, MRCP in
    conjunction with the Superintendent of Domestic Subjects, Marian E Cuff,
    on *A Course of Meals given to Necessitous Children from April to July,
    1907* original copy in the National Archives.

School feeding went through various stages in the 20th century. Initially local authorities were only allowed to charge for the basic cost of the ingredients, but by 1957 this had changed and they could charge extra on top of this for preparing and serving food. This in turn paved the way for outsourcing of school meals contracts to private providers, and a deregulation of nutritional standards by the 1980s. We won't rehearse the entire 2005 Jamie Oliver and 34% meat Turkey Twizzler debate here, in which catering companies such as Scolarest were exposed for poor standards and high profit margins, but we do need to explore the wider context of child nutrition in relation to risk. As we have moved from weight gain and growth being a primary motivation a century ago to weight loss and overall nutritional standards being a policy driver now, the food landscape for children has changed dramatically and with it their physical shape.

It's possible to track these concerns in relation to children's health over time through the medical research literature. In the late 1990s and early 2000s, we see an increasing number of academic papers arguing that environmental factors were leading to obesogenic lifestyles, and this was having an impact on children's health. Aviva Must and Richard Strauss published research looking at the medical consequences of obesity as well as issues such as self-esteem, and the later economic impact of children being overweight.[19] Researchers Cara Ebbeling, Dorota Pawlak and David Ludwig saw childhood obesity as a public health crisis requiring a common-sense but politically difficult cure, through encouraging parenting and lifestyle changes.[20] During this period, there were also attempts to track trends internationally. Scientists struggled at first to develop a universal definition of childhood obesity, but they eventually saw a link between countries in which there was greater urbanisation, and a higher likelihood of children being obese (for example the work of Youfa Wang and Tim Lobstein, which looked at worldwide childhood obesity trends in depth[21]).

19 Must, A., and Strauss, R. S. (1999) 'Risk and consequences of childhood and adolescent obesity.' *International Journal of Obesity*, 23: S2-S11.
20 Ebbeling, C. B., Pawlak, D. B., and Ludwig, D. S. (2002) 'Childhood obesity: public-health crisis, common sense cure.' *The Lancet*, 360(9331) 10 August: pp. 473-482.
21 Wang, Y. and Lobstein, T. (2006) 'Worldwide trends in childhood overweight and obesity.' *Paediatric Obesity*, 1(1): pp. 11-25.

Other researchers looked at the role of obesity in early life (for example John Reilly and colleagues[22]) and it became clear that the years before the age of three were crucial in determining a child's risk of obesity – what some researchers started calling the 'first 1000 days' approach. Reilly and colleagues found that risk factors here for very young children included early raised BMI; eight hours or more television watching a week; high weight gain the first year; high birth weight; and sleep deprivation (which they defined as 10.5 hours or fewer a night). These are all indicative of the early areas of research.

More recently a shift in research emphasis has taken place. Solveig Cunningham and colleagues built on the 'first 1000 days' research, finding that a lot of the damage is done in early childhood, and if children are overweight or obese at the age of three, then the chances of them remaining so later on is higher (and they found roughly half of American children had been overweight at some stage).[23] Patricia Cheung and colleagues found in a systematic review of the wider research literature that the older the children were, the less likely they were to be overweight. It was clear that children were starting to slim down over time, statistically speaking.[24] This tied in with research carried out by Wabitsch and colleagues, which indicated an unexpected plateau of childhood obesity rates in developed countries. They attributed this to an increase in physical activity, a decline in TV viewing, a decline in the consumption of soft, fizzy drinks, and the overall cumulative effect of public health programmes.[25] If this plateau continues, the childhood

---

22 Reilly, J., Armstrong, J., Dorosty, A., Emmett, P., Ness, A., Rogers, I., Steer, C., Sherriff, A. (2005) 'Early life risk factors for obesity in childhood: cohort study.' *British Medical Journal*, 330(7504): p. 1357.

23 Cunningham, S. A., Kramer, M. R., and Venkat Narayan, K. M. (2014) 'Incidence of childhood obesity in the United States.' *New England Journal of Medicine*, 360: pp. 403-411.

24 Cheung, P. C., Cunningham, S. A., Venkat Narayan, K. M., Kramer, M. R. (2016) 'Childhood obesity in the United States: A systematic review.' *Childhood Obesity*, 12(1): pp. 1-11.

25 Wabitsch, M., Moss, A., and Kromeyer-Hauschild, K. (2014) 'Unexpected plateauing of childhood obesity rates in developed countries.' *BMC Medicine*, 12(17).

obesity crisis may well be an example of one moral panic where alarmist statements may have been justified and certainly may have led to some medical and social good.

Online pornography

Internet pornography also inspires a great deal of concern. Yet, as with childhood obesity, the focus of research has changed gradually over time. Early studies by researchers such as Sonia Livingstone and Magdalena Bober[26] and the 2008 Byron Review[27] were frequently based on sources such as surveys of parents and teachers carried out by polling organisations, and polling of academic experts, in which it was said that 20-25% of children had encountered pornography online (this varied a little according to the age group and country being polled). This early research led in turn to highly vocal demands for internet service providers to provide filtering services, as seen in the expert report produced for the UK's Department of Culture, Media and Sport by Nash and colleagues, although this was qualified by a concern that over-surveillance may lead to unintended consequences such as greater use of peer-to-peer sharing of potentially harmful materials via social media (something which wasn't in widespread use around 2004, or at least not in the way we use it now).[28]

More recent research warns that a blanket approach to surveillance and filtering may not be the only answer. In an Australian study, Shelley Walker, Meredith Temple-Smith, Peter Higgs and Lena Sanci argued that internet pornography is now largely inescapable for many teens.

---

26   See Livingstone, S., and Bober, M. (2004) *UK children go online: Surveying the experiences of young people and their parents.* London, LSE Research Online. Available at: https://eprints.lse.ac.uk/ archive/00000395 (Accessed: 6 August 2021).

27   See Byron, T. (2008) *Safer children in a digital world: The report of the Byron Review.* Independent report. www.iwf.org.uk/sites/default/files/ inline-files/Safer%20Children%20in%20a%20Digital%20World%20 report.pdf

28   Nash, V. et al. (2015) *Identifying the routes by which children view pornography online: implications for future policymakers seeking to limit viewing.* Report of the Expert Panel for the UK Department of Culture, Media and Sport. London: HMSO.

They found that it was viewed both intentionally and unintentionally, but engagement with pornography could sometimes be reflective, for example with concern for the negative portrayal of relationships and women.[29] Tony Lawson and Chris Comber argue that internet censorship, in this case in schools, was only ever likely to be a partial solution to any problem, and that it was necessary to alert pupils systematically to potential dangers, as well as encouraging responsible use (something that had also been encouraged in studies such as the 2008 Byron review).[30] Other researchers were trying to see internet pornography in a more positive light, in the context of wider social change. Andrew Hope makes a very important point in his work about the way the adult narrative surrounding pornography viewing changes depending upon the age of the children concerned. Younger teens are often seen as innocents being corrupted, whereas older teens (perhaps post-puberty) are often seen as having passed through some sort of moral threshold and are deliberately engaging in something harmful. Which narrative applies at any particular time seems to depend on a moral judgement on the part of the adult concerned,[31] in the way we described in the previous chapter and classifications of childhood.

There has also been research into the extent of any potential harm for adolescents. Here there aren't may conclusive findings, but the general feeling is that it may have a negative effect on self-concept. On the other hand, researchers such as Eric Owens, Richard Behun, Jill Manning and Rory Reid, in an extensive review of the current research, found that pornography use declines as teenagers become more confident in themselves. Nevertheless, there are still some significant areas of risk here, which include lower degrees of social integration, increases in behaviour problems and delinquency, increasing depression, and lower

---

29 Walker, S., Temple-Smith, M., Higgs, P., and Sanci, L. (2015) 'It's always just there in your face.' *Sexual Health*, 12(3): pp. 200-206.

30 Lawson, T., and Comber, C. (2010) 'Censorship, the Internet and schools: a new moral panic?' *The Curriculum Journal*, 2000, 11(2): pp. 273-285.

31 Hope, A. (2006) 'School Internet use, youth and risk: a socio-cultural study of the relation between staff views of online dangers and pupils' ages in UK schools.' *British Educational Research Journal*, 32(2): pp. 307-329.

levels of closeness with parents and other carers.[32] At the fringes of the research are papers usually based on quite small studies. For example, Mark McCormack and Liam Wignall suggest it's simply a harmless leisure time activity for older teen boys,[33] but studies such as this don't always take into account the addictive nature of internet images, and the consequential effects of engagement in the medium to long term (we go into this in more depth in a later chapter, including the impact of gender on sexting behaviours).

Where does this leave us as adults meant to be guiding children? We probably have to accept that internet pornography is here to stay, although it takes different forms over time, and it will flow through any surveillance cracks like water. Whether it damages our children is likely to come down to the quality of the conversation we can have with them about it, like everything else, and how carefully we educate them to recognise the fiction that is the perfect body or sexual relationship, as presented online.

Drugs

There is currently a record number of exclusions taking place relating to drug and alcohol use in UK schools, with 12,180 permanent and fixed-term exclusions taking place in 2018-2019, the most recent year for which there was data at the time of writing.[34] This is now significantly more likely than tobacco smoking among secondary-school pupils. A 2016 NHS England survey[35] found that, in the UK at any rate, 19% of

---

32   Owens, E.W., Behun, R. J., Manning, J. C., and Reid, R. C. (2012) 'The impact of internet pornography on adolescents: A review of the research.' *Sexual Addiction and Compulsivity*, 19: pp. 99-122.

33   McCormack, M., and Wignall, L. (2016) 'Enjoyment, exploration and education: Understanding the consumption of pornography among young men with non-exclusive sexual orientations.' *Sociology*, 51(5): pp. 975-991.

34   Department for Education. (2020) *Permanent and fixed-period exclusions in England: 2018 to 2019*. Available at: www.gov.uk/government/statistics/permanent-and-fixed-period-exclusions-in-england-2018-to-2019 (Accessed: 6 August 2021).

35   NHS Digital (2016) *Smoking, drinking and drug use among young people* Available at: www.digital.nhs.uk/catalogue/PUB30132 (Accessed: 5 August 2021).

pupils aged 11-15 had smoked, 24% had taken drugs, and 44% had drunk alcohol. Therefore we have to ask ourselves – does this too represent another worthwhile moral panic?

Like so much to do with assessing risks among adolescents, a lot of perceived risk here is in the eye of the beholder, and it is important to scale our concern. There is a great deal of difference between a 15-year-old having a bravado puff on a friend's cigarette and an 11-year-old being a regular smoker. Having an occasional swig of a beer at a family barbeque is very different from routinely drinking spirits every weekend. Drugs also range in toxicity and addictive impact, as well as criminalisation potential.[36] Therefore it is important to bear this in mind when considering how worried to be. The NHS data helpfully distinguish between regular use and occasional experimentation, to a certain extent. The main issue, however, is whether overall use is going down over time. If we compare the data to that of 2004, the earliest digital document readily available, we can see that the rates were 39% for smoking (more than double), 59% for alcohol (much higher) and 26% for drugs (a little higher). Therefore things are on the right track, but drug use rates seem to be reducing more slowly than the other measures (bear in mind this also includes things like legal highs, glue sniffing, nitrous oxide, and so on, phenomena that sometimes put the rates up temporarily). These findings are similar to those in other studies, for example Jay Penney and colleagues, who found a decline among the 15-18 age group in London.[37]

If things are gradually improving, therefore, do we need to be worried? Sometimes the issue is more environmental. There might be a perceived threat, or it might be an actual one. For example, in terms of a perceived threat, parents sometimes talk about 'bad areas', where drugs are rife. In Britain, there is also great concern about 'county lines' drug gangs, where criminal syndicates use vulnerable children and young people to

---

36   See the Talk to Frank drugs education website for more information. www.talktofrank.com/faq/what-drug-classification-system
37   Penney, J., Dargan, P. I., Padmore, J., Wood, D. M., and Norman, I. J. (2016) 'Epidemiology of adolescent substance use in London Schools.' *QJM: An International Journal of Medicine*, 109(6): pp. 405-409.

transport drugs via organised routes.[38] However, Martin found in relation to US neighbourhoods that as they became gentrified, this kind of fear of drug dealing had more to do with 'othering' of community members from different backgrounds rather than a quantifiably increased risk of young people being sold drugs locally. This distinction was often done on grounds of ethnicity, perhaps manifesting itself as a form of racism felt to be more acceptable in some way by incomers.[39] On the other hand, risks may be where you least expect them. A US study by Atav and Spencer, which looked at 2000 young people, found that there were important differences in the levels of risky behaviour between urban and rural adolescents, so this can also represent a potential geographical factor.[40] Of course, these are not English or UK studies, but they do give us an indication of some of the nuances that might apply. For wealthier pupils, they sometimes deploy drugs to help with school performance, as found in a Swiss study by Evangelia Liakoni and colleagues. Tools in the pupil's homework arsenal appear to include energy drinks (indeed NHS England has started to collect data on this as well), coffee, tobacco, and methylphenidate drugs (usually prescribed for certain forms of ADHD but sometimes available as 'street' drugs; the most usual formulation is Ritalin).[41] Even just the physical act of going to school can be risky, as we see in a US study by Milam and colleagues, who found that simply the act of walking past an alcohol outlet increased the risk of adolescents using alcohol.[42]

---

38 www.nationalcrimeagency.gov.uk/who-we-are/publications/257-county-lines-drug-supply-vulnerability-and-harm-2018/file

39 Martin, L. (2008) 'Boredom, drugs, and schools: Protecting children in gentrifying communities.' *City and Community*, 7(4): pp. 331-346.

40 Atav, S., and Spencer, G. A. (2002) 'Health risk behaviours among adolescents attending rural, suburban and urban schools: A comparative study.' *Family and Community Health*, 25(2): pp. 53-64.

41 Liakoni, E. et al. (2015) 'The use of prescription drugs, recreational drugs, and "soft enhancers" for cognitive enhancement among Swiss secondary school students.' *PLoS One*, 10(10).

42 Milam, A. J., Furr-Holden, C. D. M., Cooley-Strickland, M. C., Bradshaw, C. P., and Leaf, P. J. (2013) 'Risk for exposure to alcohol, tobacco, and other drugs on the route to and from school: The role of alcohol outlets.' *Preventative Science*, 15(1): pp. 12-21.

Of course, over the years there have been many school-based interventions, but these are not always as effective as we might like them to be. A Dutch evaluation by Monique Malmberg and colleagues found that local interventions there hadn't really worked.[43] So, what does work? We know that government legislation makes a big difference. For example, strict regulations on tobacco sales and use have reduced smoking dramatically among all age groups. This book is about how to understand issues at a more personal level, however. What can we do there? The answer is that it depends on what and who you are talking about.

For children in deprived communities, tobacco is going to be the biggest risk, and making sure smoking at home isn't normalised will make a big difference here. For adolescents in general, alcohol is potentially a problem once parents are not supervising, and here it makes sense to de-mystify, perhaps by explaining things like how much alcohol a young body can take before it starts having serious, life-threatening problems, and the problems that come with mixing drinks and not knowing exactly how much you have had. In terms of drugs, the more affluent the family, the more drugs adolescents are likely to be able to buy, so it makes sense to keep a close eye on financial flow (and whether any low-key dealing might be happening). Novel substances such as legal highs, nitrous oxide and so on are particularly difficult to anticipate and once again, even though we may be starting to be repetitive, it is here that keeping the metaphorical door open for a high quality, non-judgemental adult/child conversation might be at its most valuable. If you don't know what's going on, and you haven't done your homework, how can you possibly be in a position to advise when asked?

Radicalisation
In discussing Alan Kurdi and the way he was depicted by the world's media lying drowned on a beach, we've already talked about the power of visual imagery when it comes to our feelings about children. It is as though seeing disturbing images of children taps into a collective

---

43   Malmberg, M. et al. (2014) 'Effectiveness of the "healthy school and drugs" prevention programme on adolescents' substance use: A randomised clustered trial.' *Addiction*, 109(6): pp. 1031-1040.

parenting hive mind, unsettling us and distressing us as one. Another less emotive, but nonetheless haunting, visual image in recent years is the 2015 CCTV still of 16-year-old schoolgirl Kadiza Sultana and her 15-year-old friends walking through security at Gatwick Airport before boarding Turkish Airlines flight TK1966 for Istanbul, en route to Raqqa in Syria. Kadiza was travelling in the company of two other girls from her school, Bethnal Green Academy, during the February half term prior to sitting her GCSEs, in which she was expected to achieve straight A grades. (The school was regarded as one of the top-performing state schools in the country.) Their aim was to join the organisation known commonly as Islamic State, or Daesh. (Since then, one of the girls, Shamima Begum, has been found and become the focus of a diplomatic fight over whether she should be allowed to retain her UK passport. She married a Dutch Islamic convert and gave birth to three children, all of whom have died.)

You may notice we are trying to keep our language as neutral as possible in this section. When seeking to understand phenomena such as these, there are key themes appearing repeatedly in reporting and debates, with often morally-loaded terminology used fairly loosely as a shorthand for another moral panic. In media stories surrounding Kadiza's flight to Syria, and subsequent stories about Shamima's return, for example, we repeatedly see words that have become familiar to us over the last two decades: 'radicalisation', 'jihadists', 'grooming', 'extremism'. At the root of the use of these words lies uncertainty, and a collective sense that something is out of control and threatening the equilibrium of society. It comes across as something of a discourse of despair.

Academics Vicki Coppock and Mark McGovern, from Edge Hill University in the UK, have written about how we might need to start challenging the assumptions inherent in the use of this language, if we are to understand precisely how best to tackle it.[44] They discuss the

---

44   Coppock, V., and McGovern, M. (2014) '"Dangerous minds"?
     Deconstructing counter-terrorism discourse, radicalisation and the
     "psychological vulnerability" of Muslim children and young people in
     Britain.' *Children and Society*, 28(3): pp. 242-256.

UK Government's 'Prevent'[45] policy and 'Channel'[46] programme, both aimed at taking pre-emptive steps to avoid terrorist involvement. For readers unfamiliar with these UK Government initiatives, 'Prevent' is a referral scheme whereby professionals such as teachers, social workers and lecturers are required to report those individuals they consider to be at risk of radicalisation (this is not just concerned with Islamic fundamentalism, but can also include involvement with far-right organisations, and indeed recently the government was careful to point out that in 2016-2017 one third of referrals were made on this basis).[47] 'Channel' is described by a Channel Intervention Provider in a government press release as a 'voluntary and confidential safeguarding programme which provides support to people identified as vulnerable to being drawn into terrorism. It deals with all forms of radicalisation including Islamist extremism and the extreme right-wing'. Both of these initiatives come under the umbrella of the government's anti-terrorist CONTEST[48] strategy.

Coppock and McGovern raise important points about how the use of language shows that various societal issues have been conflated here within government policy, which is problematic for the future of such policies and practices. Firstly they argue that there is a particular conception of childhood that is grounded in the idea of children as being

45 HM Government. (2011) *Prevent Strategy*. Available at www.gov.uk/government/uploads/system/uploads/attachment_data/file/97976/prevent-strategy-review.pdf (Accessed: 6 August 2021).

46 HM Government. (2012) *Channel: Protecting vulnerable people from being drawn into terrorism*. London: HM Government.

47 UK Government. (2018) *New figures show improved referrals to Prevent and a rise in far-right concerns*. Press Release issued 27 March 2018. Available at: www.gov.uk/government/news/new-figures-show-improved-referrals-to-prevent-and-a-rise-in-far-right-concerns (Accessed: 6 August 2021).

48 HM Government. (2011) *CONTEST: The United Kingdom's strategy for countering terrorism*. (HM Government, London) Available at: https://assets.publishing.service.gov.uk/government/uploads/system/uploads/attachment_data/file/97994/contest-summary.pdf (Accessed: 6 August 2021).

vulnerable, something we covered in chapter 1. This allows everything to come under the umbrella of 'child protection' or 'safeguarding' as a concept. As we've argued ourselves earlier in this chapter, it's very difficult to formulate arguments successfully stating that children need to be less safe, which accounts for the ready co-opting of the term as a means of legitimising what is being done. They then explain that it is linked to ideas of the 'New Terrorism' (presumably in contrast to old forms of terrorism in a pre-social media age, whatever they might be), with Muslims disproportionately affected, as they are informally and crudely profiled while going about their everyday lives. It makes it easy for certain children to be labelled without any useful recourse.

The authors then criticise the general idea underpinning government anti-terrorism policies, in which radicalisation is seen as a tidy, sequential process with distinct phases, when active intervention may be seen as deflecting individuals from a negative life path. While this may have considerable appeal in terms of creating apparent order from chaos, it runs the risk of making things worse by generating too many false positives, where innocent young citizens going about their everyday lives are targeted unnecessarily. This is made very clear in the comparable European Union study into the prevention of radicalisation, which emphasises the need for nuanced approaches, as well as making clear that the wrong approach could be very damaging.[49] We have both undertaken compulsory Prevent training as part of our university jobs, and we were struck by how vague the criteria for referral were, and how they might apply to the majority of adolescents at one time or another. For example, *'may begin with a search for answers to questions about identity, faith and belonging'* could be seen as the entire *raison d'être* of children's psychological development after primary school. *'May be driven by the desire for "adventure and excitement"'* describes anyone who has had a modicum of ambition to see the world, or been on a Duke of Edinburgh trip. *'May be driven by a desire to enhance the self-esteem of the individual and promote their "street cred"'* once again reminds us both of how a great deal of our headspace was primarily occupied during our own teen years.

---

49   Bigo, D., Bonelli, L., Guittet, E-P., and Ragazzi, F. (2014) *Preventing and countering youth radicalisation in the EU*. Brussels: European Union.

In fact, this pathologising of vague attributes common to many individuals may also have the effect of muting important forms of dissent, as explored in the research of Liverpool academics Gabe Mythen, Sandra Walklate and Elizabeth-Jane Peatfield.[50] During this act of silencing, they argue, the government seeks to disrupt something that is essentially unpredictable in terms of its progression, an act that is in many cases going to be futile because it has no logical path (a point also made in the EU report). This is because the Prevent policy is primarily based upon the notion that individuals are rational actors, who at some point are potentially corrupted ('groomed') by dangerous ideologies. In this context, argue the authors, actively voicing criticism of government foreign policy and any relationship to its own atrocities becomes difficult if not impossible for certain minority ethnic groups, for fear of being labelled. Researchers Stijn Sieckelinck, Femke Kaulingfreks and Micha de Winter describe this as a 'villain/victim' way of framing situations.[51] In sociology generally, we call this a process of 'othering', where certain groups of people are seen as being outside the mainstream and treated adversely. In their article, Mythen, Walklate and Peatfield give the oft-cited example of a 16-year-old referred to Prevent for taking out a library book on terrorism, and a four-year-old boy who had allegedly drawn a picture of a bomb-making 'cooking pot'. In both cases, children have been 'othered' for doing things that in other contexts might have been perfectly acceptable. As social work researchers Tony Stanley and Surinder Guru point out, 'risk factors get counted up and (too easily) simplistically conflated to high risk. This is a problem for families and for [social work] practice'.[52] Indeed, in researching this very chapter we drew on library materials relating to terrorism ourselves, and in the 1970s we watched the anarchic television cartoon *Road Runner* regularly,

---

50 Gabe, M., Walklate, S., and Peatfield, E-J. (2017) 'Assembling and deconstructing radicalisation in PREVENT: A case of policy-based evidence making?' *Critical Social Policy*, 37(2): pp. 180-201.

51 Sieckelinck, S., Kaulingfreks, F., and De Winter, M. (2015) 'Neither villains nor victims: Towards an educational perspective on radicalisation.' *British Journal of Educational Studies*, 63(3): pp. 329-343.

52 Stanley, T., and Guru, S. (2015) 'Childhood radicalisation risk: An emerging practice issue.' *Practice*, 27(5): pp. 353-366.

which featured the magnificently anthropomorphised Wile E. Coyote using diverse and exciting ACME bombs to blow up characters (and sometimes himself) at every possible opportunity, something which no doubt featured in our own action drawings at the age of four. Hopefully there won't be a knock on the door.

Data privacy rights

Our final moral panic looks at the role of children's data privacy rights in contemporary society. This particular moral panic began with the introduction of easily affordable and accessible digital photography in the mid-2000s, and slightly later with the widespread adoption of social media accounts.

The first indicator of the moral panic took place in schools. For a few years, the newspapers were full of stories about how parents had been banned from taking pictures of their children during Nativity plays and at school sports days, on the grounds of 'data protection' and 'safeguarding', even though this had no grounds in law and made no sense in terms of risk assessments. Sandra remembers attending a leaving party given in 2005 at a nursery one of her children attended, and being told she could only take pictures from an odd angle of her own child, and not of any of his friends, something that was stringently and vigorously policed on the day.

The fuss about photographing children got so out of hand at one stage, that the UK Information Commissioner's Office was forced to issue official guidance stating that taking pictures of children at school events was legally permissible. Yet at the same time, schools were perfectly happy to break the law themselves by coercing children to have their fingerprints taken for biometric lunch cards, or featuring them in school publicity shots, without the permission of their parents. This was not legally permissible then, and since the 2018 introduction of the General Data Protection Regulation (GDPR) across Europe, the situation is even clearer now. Without parental permission, pictures and biometrics can only be collected for very particular uses and where no alternative can be provided, for example to attach a picture of a pupil to a file in the school office so members of staff can identify individuals. There isn't usually a distinct use for biometrics that can't be achieved equally well via the use of a swipe card, something we will come back to later. Hence biometrics should always be optional in schools, as those of us sitting on the Privacy Expert Group of the Biometrics Institute continually state in our best practice guidelines. Indeed, in countries such as France and Germany they are banned in such situations.

There are a number of reasons that schools habitually get the issue of permission wrong. For some schools, the distinction between parents being able to decide how they take pictures of their children on school sites, but schools not having the same rights, can be genuinely confusing and counter-intuitive, and arises from a relatively poor understanding of data protection law. For other schools, preventing parents (and children) from doing everyday things can be a form of control, a darker means of ensuring parents and pupils are on the back foot and subject to the head teacher's interpretation of what is allowed (the same mindset that results in head teachers measuring the length of school skirts on teenage females to determine what is 'acceptable'). This control represents a kind of power imbalance, resulting in the rather sad outcome of children being deprived of recording their social histories – perhaps a starring role as a Nativity angel, or a memorable sports team win – with little or no recourse. (We urge head teachers to reflect on this issue, as we consider a collaborative leadership model is likely to have more positive long-term effects than a combative one.)

Yet before the National Association of Head Teachers protests that we've got it all wrong, this is not just an issue of whether a small minority of head teachers has historically been overly controlling. Children's data privacy rights are an important indicator of what is happening, or about to happen, in the rest of society in terms of surveillance and monitoring, so it's particularly interesting to explore them in detail. School children have significant contact with bureaucracy on a daily basis, and consequently they may be held hostage to unethical policies and practices in a more extensive sense than just school, by their very need to secure an education.

For example, data collection by the authorities about children can be intense and comprehensive. During an English child's school career, he or she will be included in a large number of computer databases, with and sometimes without parental consent, and this has come about for several reasons. The main reason is that the increasing affordability of high-level computer processing power has made it comparatively simple to store and manipulate vast quantities of data. The following table lists some of the child-related databases in existence over the last two decades or so. There are also databases held by the police and health services, and sometimes these are cross-referenced. However, the table lists those in which teachers and school administrators have been responsible for data entry.

Database	Frequency	Date	Nature of data
Pupil Level Annual School Census ('PLASC'), from 2007 National Pupil Database and Termly Pupil School Census	Annually until 2007, then termly (first Thursday in January, May and October)	1998 to date	Home postcode School Social deprivation measures Age Ethnicity Gender Pupil attainment Special Educational Needs Educational history
ContactPoint	Ongoing	2004-10	Name, address, gender and date of birth Pupil Identification Number Name and contact details of parents/ guardians Educational history GP details Other service provider details Information about any causes for concern Other categories of information as specified from time to time by Secretary of State (e.g. substance or alcohol abuse by parents, family lifestyle, household expenditure)
Vetting and Barring Scheme	Abandoned	2010	Individual identification of over-18s Criminal records Police cautions

Database	Frequency	Date	Nature of data
Ofsted	Periodically	1991 to date	Compliance with government education and welfare policies Personally identifiable information of adults (Home childcarers) Names and ages of children being cared for (Home childcarers)
Attendance data	Twice daily	1870 to date	Individual identification of pupils Attendance/absence
Admissions data	Annually	1870 to date	Individual identification of pupils Age, home address, method of transport to school, names of parents/ guardians.

Table 1: School-related educational databases

The aim of this monitoring, which involves such extensive data being captured and stored, is often put forward as a method of increasing public sector efficiency, effectiveness, reliability and accountability. It is also sometimes used as a covert indicator of how thorough and professional certain teachers and governments are – the more monitoring the better. However, it also raises serious questions about the nature of the data being captured and processed. Some is genuinely useful, for example seeing where children are living and whether they are on site that day, whereas other forms of data collection are more questionable, such as using their fingerprints or facial recognition systems.

This is particularly the case when schools collect fingerprints from children. This type of biometric data collection is not just confined to school dinners and taking out library books, of course. It also takes place in the commercial sector. Sandra was intrigued to see a holiday park in Suffolk recently collecting children's fingerprints so they could buy action shots of themselves on the slides in the swimming pool. However, this kind of thing is rarer in the private rather than public domain. (Incidentally, children's fingerprints are not yet fully formed and sometimes almost identical in machine-readable form, plus wet fingers don't read very well on the biometric pad, so this was an ill-advised choice of identity management in the light of long queues of soaking wet children trying to make the gadget work. Perhaps the holiday park has realised that now.) The former Children's Commissioner, Anne Longfield, issued a report on this kind of proliferation of children's personal data gathering entitled *Who knows what about me,*[53] which indicates it is becoming an increasing concern.

A lack of transparency and accountability in terms of data processing by schools and commercial companies hasn't helped, which is why the GDPR was felt to be necessary, so that individuals had more control over this, although in reality the situation can be complex and difficult at times. For example, social media participation is notionally optional in society, but in schools, pupils may be coercively subjected to such technologies, for example being expected to log onto YouTube in order to look at homework videos, or digital classroom platforms in order to participate in online lessons during remote teaching periods as a result of the Covid-19 pandemic. Shaped by these online structures, children's learning may start to be tailored more and more closely to what is expected of those technologies. In other words, if arithmetic or vocabulary recall is easy to measure electronically, this may become a mainstay of primary school homework rather than individual mathematical projects. In time, it may even become the focus of artificial intelligence education systems for children in state-maintained schools that find themselves on a restricted budget. On the other hand, carefully crafted teaching provided by a human and only supported in the background by artificial intelligence tools, would come at a premium, and may end up being the predominant model in an independent sector aimed at affluent parents.

If you imagine this trend towards electronic data gathering about children combined with politics, you can even see a situation in which gathering children's data becomes potentially dangerous in the hands of an authoritarian state, although to be fair we are not expecting to see anything like this happen in Europe in the foreseeable future. We have, however, seen China using similar information for its Social Credit Score to keep track of the trustworthiness of its 1.3 billion citizens (or indeed whether they hold views in opposition to those of the Chinese state). In

---

53 www.childrenscommissioner.gov.uk/publication/who-knows-what-about-me/

an extreme political context, if this approach were to be used on children, there is a great deal of scope for manipulation of the developing mind in ways that might have adverse consequences later on.

Will we ever go down such a path? We don't imagine this would happen deliberately, but it might happen accidentally, given the extensive nature of commercial involvement in schools in the UK and US. It may happen by the back door, through databases being sold and cross-referenced. Indeed, we gave written evidence to the UK's Department for Education in 2012 to this effect, explaining that it was technically already possible to cross-reference children's data to such a degree that individuals could be identified and potentially disadvantaged.[54] This is not something either of us would like to see happening.

Luckily the GDPR is something of a knight in shining armour in this regard. There are several important aspects to the regulation which will help schools tread the ethical path:

- Age of consent – The age of consent for the use of personal data has effectively dropped from 16 to 13 in some cases, for example in relation to social media, although this is highly variable and culturally specific, so still depends on the territory to some extent. While this means children may be less mature when they provide consent, we are at least moving towards a consistent age threshold that may be more easily understood across the European region (and perhaps internationally).

- Age verification – It is still very difficult to define the identity of a child as opposed to a parent online, and this is something of a technological holy grail. This hasn't been resolved, but it nevertheless still appears in the GDPR, perhaps as a kind of triumph of hope over experience. In the meantime, schools can work with children so they improve their abilities to self-regulate

---

54   Department for Education. (2012) *Proposed amendments to individual pupil information prescribed persons regulations.* Available at: www. openrightsgroup.org/app/uploads/2020/03/consultation-document-on-proposed-amendments-to-individual-pupil-information-prescribed-persons-regulations.pdf (Accessed: 25 August 2021).

online. This should be part of any contemporary school's Personal, Social, Citizenship and Health Education programme.

- Transparency – This is an important term in the GDPR. This is because the majority of interactions on the internet are not particularly transparent, so it represents an attempt to force companies and organisations to be more honest about the data they collect and what they use it for. Here schools may be obliged to be more precise about the intended use of data they collect. For example, it would not be acceptable to collect fingerprints for a school meals biometric system, and then use that database to identify culprits who have been throwing empty crisp packets around the school premises instead of placing them in the waste bin, however tempting this might be.

- Accountability – This is another very important term. Organisations are not just required to comply, but they also have to demonstrate how they comply. With the transparency objective, this effectively acts as a form of social engineering, because the regulators considered things hadn't gone far enough previously, meaning people couldn't always exercise their fundamental privacy rights. In terms of how this might affect schools, there needs to be a privacy-friendly mindset rather than putting the school's convenience at the centre of operations, and pupils and their parents need to be informed of their privacy rights. The consequences of getting this wrong are serious, with fines of up to 20 million euros at stake, although a more realistic outcome for schools would be to be told to stop handling data immediately – something that would make day-to-day operations almost impossible, which means compliance is of the utmost importance.

- Right to be forgotten – If it is thought that an individual's data privacy rights outweigh the public interest in publishing information about them, then the individual can ask for the information to be deleted. This will be particularly useful for teenagers and pupils who have posted things they might regret or been tagged in pictures without their permission.

How can parents navigate the modern world of risk?

It's important to remember that life is getting safer all the time, despite the impression given to us by rolling news services and social media platforms. Children are healthier and living longer than ever before. However, the 21st century is nevertheless an anxious time in which to live. Moral panic is all around us, and it is becoming harder and harder to discriminate between likely and unlikely dangers. We hope to a certain extent, that this chapter has given a few useful indicators.

We've identified eight areas of moral panic that concern contemporary parents and explored their roots as well as whether it is necessary to take account of them in planning everyday life. We argued that teen witchcraft, for example, has softened over the years from a lifestyle that could result in the execution of individuals, to a relatively transient phenomenon that potentially encourages a gentle interest in the environment combined with fashion trends. We've discussed the need for quality over quantity when engaging with computer games, and the importance of parents understanding gaming through playing them sometimes, preferably in conjunction with young people. We've hopefully reassured some parents that it really is fine to let children play outside with their friends, as long as they avoid the traffic and things like building sites, as stranger danger is such a negligible risk it's barely worth giving much attention to in the everyday scheme of things. Conversely, we have identified obesity as a real threat to the health and wellbeing of children and young people, and encouraged parents and schools to take this a lot more seriously. (Like many other professionals, we would like to see children and young people taking at least an hour's daily exercise, preferably even two, and ditching snacks and junk food.) Online porn has been discussed in the light of the need for body confidence and a realistic understanding of how ordinary people look. Schools can do a lot of good here by being more frank about human development from an early age, and also communicating and demonstrating how it is possible to doctor images to make them look better than they are in real life. We've discussed illegal drugs, and the importance of creating an environment at home and in the area immediately around schools where alcohol, tobacco and drugs generally do not feature very prominently, so use and abuse isn't normalised in any way. Radicalisation was a difficult area to write about, as it is incredibly fraught, but we have emphasised the importance of avoiding racist categorisations and the dangers of leaping to conclusions about everyday behaviour, something the government has been aware of in its more recent reports. Finally, we have talked about data protection, and how parents and teachers need to be fully aware of the data privacy rights of children and young people, if they are to grow up in a positive, healthy society where they are valued as individuals rather than data points.

In summary, our primary advice to parents and their teachers is that it is often the really frequent risks that are taken for granted in life, such as traffic, bouncy castles and trampolines. These routinely harm and occasionally kill children and young people. However, it is the less likely risks we seem to focus on, such as the vanishingly remote possibility of being bombed when out at a concert or abducted from outside the local shop or from the local park mid-afternoon. A modern parent needs to take a more pragmatic approach to risk, balancing likelihood of a really adverse outcome with potential severity. That way, children and parents can find freedom again.

Chapter 3
'There be monsters online'

In 2019, academics at the Oxford Internet Institute published a report of a scientific study that considered the impact of social media on young people's wellbeing.[55] The report concluded that there was little evidence to suggest that social media had a wide ranging and serious impact upon the wellbeing of young people. This was, at the time, a piece of work that railed against public opinion, underpinned by government rhetoric[56] that surely the indicators of a rise in mental health issues among young people must be linked to social media use and screen time. After all, there were fewer concerns around young people's mental health in the pre-internet age. Even though the evidence was plain to see (albeit with some appreciation of statistics and data analysis), most people seemed to disagree with the findings. The general view of those choosing to ignore the reporting of the factual analysis was that it was 'obvious' that social media had a negative impact on young people. This was because, through their own anecdotal experiences, they had decided that young people in their lives were definitely unhappier than they used to be, and they use social media more. Therefore, 'obviously', it was social media's fault that they were unhappy. Other commentators went as far as to suggest that the research was 'evidence' that one should ignore what is reported in scientific journals. It would seem that if accurate analysis of data contradicts one's own views, it is perfectly acceptable to reject the findings.

---

55   Orben, A., Dienlin, T., & Przybylski, A. K. (2019) 'Social media's enduring effect on adolescent life satisfaction.' *Proceedings of the National Academy of Sciences*, 116(21): pp. 10226-10228.

56   HM Government. (2020) *The Online Harms White Paper.* Available at: www.gov.uk/government/consultations/online-harms-white-paper/online-harms-white-paper (Accessed: 6 August 2021).

While the reporting itself was not a particularly significant news story, for those of us who work in the online safeguarding area looking to develop an evidence base to inform policy and education, the story is a clear vignette in the *Post-truth* era[57] in which facts and evidence are readily dismissed in favour of opinion, which aligns with the confirmation bias[58] offered by our social media echo chambers. As McIntyre explored in his text, social media has a role to play here – the echo chambers of opinion and agreement, in spite of evidence to the contrary, are underpinned by media reporting, driven by the need for audience share and therefore reported with sensationalist headlines. Why, it seems, would we have a need for evidence when we've decided something is the case due to our own social experiences and the views of others we see online?

The role of the media in influencing public opinion has been the subject of academic debate for many years.[59] [60] [61] While the evidence evolves and therefore conclusions differ, it is generally agreed that mainstream media has some influence over public opinion. Whether this is compounded by the use of social media by news channels remains to be well understood due to the relative novelty of this approach to information consumption. While the impact of social media on lives and organisations is still only just beginning to be understood, its impact in popular culture has been significant, and concern around the impact of misinformation grows.

Misinformation in online safeguarding

Misinformation and conjecture as fact are rife within the online safeguarding world and show little sign of abating. This can be

57   McIntyre, L. (2018) *Post-truth*. Cambridge, Massachusetts: MIT Press.
58   McNeill, L. S. (2018) '"My friend posted it and that's good enough for me!": Source perception in online information sharing.' *Journal of American Folklore*, 131(522): pp. 493-499.
59   Zucker, H. G. (1978) 'The variable nature of news media influence.' *Annals of the International Communication Association*, 2(1): pp. 225-240.
60   Kozma, R. B. (1994) 'Will media influence learning? Reframing the debate.' *Educational technology research and development*, 42(2): pp. 7-19.
61   Kitzinger, J. (2004) *Framing abuse: Media influence and public understanding of sexual violence against children*. London: Pluto Press.

problematic and result in well-meaning views, formed as a result of consuming misinformation, having a poorly formed opinion about something, or a lack of critical thinking about information presented, having a negative impact upon the very young people we are claiming we wish to protect from online harms. In the early stages of the Covid-19 pandemic, the NSPCC issued a press release claiming, somewhat alarmingly, that 'Lonely children are twice as likely to be groomed online'.[62] Further exploration of the press article shows that there was also a claim that those young people who 'relied on social media' were also twice as likely to be groomed.

However, while their press release was somewhat difficult to unpick, as it does not link to the data set used or a more detailed piece of analysis, if we are to disentangle the reporting further, these claims seem somewhat flimsy. The report said this was based upon a survey where young people were asked about whether they had received or been asked to send sexual messages to an adult online, what was their social media use, etc. So, the young people were the ones who disclosed whether they felt they were 'reliant' on social media. This is a subjective interpretation at best. We have certainly worked with young people who believed they spent too much time online but, when explored further, it is clear that they are probably spending as little as an hour a day using technology. Assuming that none of the young people in the NSPCC's survey had received clinical training, reliance is something quite difficult to judge. One young person's reliance will be another's regular and healthy use.

If we are also to take the numbers at face value (because this is all we can do with no means of exploring the data set in more detail), it claims that in a sample of 2000 young people, 4% had received or been asked to send a sexual message to an adult. This would be 80 of the respondents overall. The claim that 'this more than doubled to 9% for children who felt lonely, unhappy, were extroverted and who rely on social media' would suggest that 'reliance on social media' was only disclosed by a minority of overall respondents. Even if we were to assume half of the respondents had self-

---

62   NSPCC. (2020) *Lonely children are twice as likely to be groomed* online. Available at: www.nspcc.org.uk/about-us/news-opinion/2020/coronavirus-children-groomed-online/ (Accessed: 6 August 2021).

disclosed that they were either lonely, unhappy, extroverted or relied on social media, this would still mean that approximately 90 had received or been asked to send a sexual message to an adult. Add to this that the age range for respondents is between 11 and 17, so some at the higher end of the age range might be in relationships with young adults. The headline 'Lonely children are twice as likely to be groomed online' starts to appear increasingly irresponsible given these numbers.

In the light of this, we explore misinformation and what can happen as a result of a lack of critical thinking around online safeguarding issues, and the increasing role confirmation bias and misinformation play in impacting on the judgements of those who, one would hope, have the wellbeing of young people for whom they have responsibility at heart. While we draw upon a specific research case study, we also make use of other examples to highlight the need for more insight into this area.

There have been few modern phenomena that have brought the danger of misinformation into such sharp focus as the Covid-19 pandemic. At the time of writing, the UK opposition party[63] has called for social media platforms to prevent the spreading of 'anti-vax' misinformation and reiterate the need to 'stamp out' this misinformation. The concern, understandably, being that with the hope of vaccination bringing an end to the pandemic, those making claims about the vaccine causing harm in increasingly complex forms could significantly impact on the success of any vaccination programme. They argued that there is a need for 'emergency laws' that would hold social media providers responsible should they fail to take down false stories about emerging Covid-19 vaccination programmes. Platforms, they stated, should be held financially and criminally liable if they fail in their *duty of care* to remove such information.

While the roots of both fake news and post-truth lie in politics and political rhetoric[64] (fake news, in particular, moving into the public

63   BBC. (2020) *Covid-19: Stop anti-vaccination fake news online with new law says Labour*. Available at: www.bbc.co.uk/news/uk-politics-54947661 (Accessed: 10 August 2021).
64   Rochlin, N. (2017) 'Fake news: belief in post-truth.' *Library hi tech*, 35(3): pp. 386-392.

consciousness as a result of its repeated use by politicians on both sides of the Atlantic), misinformation extends far beyond those worlds to impact upon society as a whole. The Covid-19 pandemic has rapidly increased concerns about misinformation because, frankly, misinformation about a pandemic can be incredibly dangerous. During the pandemic many examples of misinformation have surfaced via social media.[65] To look specifically at Covid-19 misinformation:

- Covid-19 is said to be fake and being used by governments to control populations.

- Covid-19 is said to be spread by the roll out of 5G networks.

- Wearing masks to prevent the spread of Covid-19 is said to reduce blood oxygen levels in the wearer.

- Covid-19 vaccines are said to alter your DNA.

- Covid-19 is allegedly being used to encourage vaccination programmes, and the vaccine contains a microchip developed by Bill Gates that will result in the mind control of the population so as to be controlled by the New World Order.

Arguably, the Covid-19 pandemic presents the perfect storm for an acceleration of misinformation due to the complexity and need for *hard* information to be able to understand it fully, resulting in the moral panics of which we have already discussed.

We have already discussed Stanley Cohen's seminal work on moral panic. He considered how media discourse can be used to fire up social concern about things of which mainstream culture has little knowledge, or where in order to clearly understand the issues there is a need for complex information. While Cohen's work centred around how *traditional* media might create panic among a population based upon the complexity of the issues, we can see parallels with digital information, and how less regulated information sources might also play a role in accelerating poorly formed public opinion. Cohen defined three core aspects of a representation of a moral panic – it must be:

---

65   Brennen, J. S., Simon, F., Howard, P. N., and Nielsen, R. K. (2020) 'Types, sources, and claims of COVID-19 misinformation.' Reuters Institute.

1. *new* (alien to the population and difficult to recognise, 'creeping up on the moral horizon'), but also *old* (relating to traditions and historical stories)
2. *damaging*, but also have *warning signs* for real danger
3. *transparent* (out in the open for everyone to see) but also *opaque*, requiring detailed explanation from experts to make people aware of the 'real harm'.

In examining the Covid-19 pandemic, this is a perfect vehicle for a moral panic:

1. While the virus itself is new, we have a history of having to deal with pandemics in the past (for example, the often quoted 'Spanish flu', not to mention the bubonic plague) and the damage they caused.
2. Clearly the early reporting on Covid-19 showed the harm in a very visual manner, in particular pictures of people on ventilators, interviews with the bereaved, and so on.
3. While there is great visibility in the media, and social media, about the impact of Covid-19, to actually understand the pandemic, epidemiology and vaccination requires detailed scientific knowledge that is complex.

As a result of the complexity, and the need for critical insight in understanding the information about the pandemic, it can be genuinely hard to make sense of the situation. After a surfeit of government briefings, ('Next slide please') we all fancy ourselves as armchair epidemiologists now. The stark reality is that the majority of the population does not receive postgraduate education in science, let alone specifically in epidemiology and public health. Official government information can therefore seem overwhelming, and this frequently results in real demand for easier answers. These can be made available quickly and easily on social media. However, social media and peer information might provide the answers *we are looking for*, rather than the answers *we need to hear*. This confirmation bias[66] can be observed

---

66   Nickerson, R. S. (1998) 'Confirmation bias: A ubiquitous phenomenon in many guises.' *Review of general psychology*, 2(2): pp. 175-220.

via social media as it provides the means to access information from any perspective on a given topic. The lack of regulation of platforms means that, within legal boundaries, users are welcome to publish whatever they wish. It does not have to be triangulated, as in traditional media, or even true. In the new frontier of the social media echo chambers[67] users will be drawn to information, regardless of factual accuracy, that will align with personal belief systems. After all, if their online friend, whom they trust, has shared information, why would they not believe it? And if it is from someone they do not know, but that person's views resonate, and they have many followers on a given platform, why would the information not be trustworthy? We may have democratised information by providing these platforms, but we have also democratised untruth.

Digital ghost stories – a post-truth phenomenon

Let us return to the focus of this book – the online world, its impact on young people, and how we can help them grow in this hyperconnected world. We have, over recent years, spent a great deal of time working with the safeguarding profession on what we might refer to as the *digital ghost story*. The digital ghost story has all of the elements of a modern moral panic and in this chapter we draw upon Cohen's theories applied to this very modern-day context. We also develop on the arguments around the differences between perceived risk and the reality of risk, as well as what can happen when professionals and those with safeguarding responsibilities for children fail to apply some critical thinking to things that arrive on their social media feeds and inboxes.

The ghost stories speak of an online phenomenon that is causing harm to young people that is difficult to understand, shared across social and traditional media, often lacking any clear evidence of actually existing. It is a new, emerging concern, but can be related to similar stories from the past. For example, the modern version involves things like a stranger contacting a child using a digital platform and encouraging them to self-

---

67   Flaxman, S., Goel, S., and Rao, J. M. (2016) 'Filter bubbles, echo chambers, and online news consumption.' *Public opinion quarterly*, 80(SI): pp. 298-320.

harm. 'Stranger danger' of this type is a well-established trope that has been played out against both offline and digital backdrops many times.

One of the earliest online digital ghost stories that was cited as causing physical harm was Slenderman, a scary meme that depicted a tall, thin, shadowy figure with no face, dressed in a black suit.[68] As sometimes happens with memes, the Slenderman story became a viral phenomenon, with fan-fiction stories posted online. These stories would generally be gruesome tales of abduction and murder carried out by the Slenderman. Eventually the Slenderman mythology was even adapted into a free-to-play video game by Parsec Productions – *Slender: The Eight Pages*.

It was perhaps the first time that online folklore was cited as a causal factor in an attempted murder by two 12-year-old girls.[69] In this case the two girls stabbed their friend, it was claimed, 'to prove Slenderman existed' and make sure he did not harm their own families. The challenge we face with online viral memes such as Slenderman is that, unless you are immersed in the mythology, it can become quite an impenetrable folklore. It is not like the days of the 'video nasty', where it was claimed certain horror movies would inspire copycat behaviour. With these movies one needed only watch it to decide whether it was harmful. One does not simply watch Slenderman to learn about it, and therefore it becomes something hidden and opaque. This makes it easier to create a mythology, as it is built around something we do not understand, and less easy to dismiss, as is a poorly made horror movie.

When the case came to trial, conjecture still attempted to suggest this Slenderman character, little more than an image on a meme site, was partly responsible. The outcome was rather more sensibly that the attackers' own mental health was the main causal factor, and both were sentenced to indefinite detention in mental health facilities. One of the perpetrators has also claimed to be conversing with Lord Voldemort and

68 Chess, S., & Newsom, E. (2015) *Folklore, horror stories, and the Slender Man: The development of an Internet mythology.* New York: Palgrave Macmillan.

69 Newsweek Magazine. (2014) *The girls who tried to kill for slender man.* Available at: www.newsweek.com/2014/08/22/girls-who-tried-kill-slender-man-264218.html (Accessed: 18 August 2021).

a Teenage Mutant Ninja Turtle. However, this was, of course, dismissed as causation because both are more readily understood in popular culture. It is far easier to dismiss something as nonsense if we understand it.

Nevertheless, a public official still used the outcome to raise concerns for parents regarding the dangers of the internet:

> 'This should be a wake-up call for all parents, the Internet has changed the way we live. It is full of information and wonderful sites that teach and entertain. The Internet can also be full of dark and wicked things.'

Returning to Cohen's moral panic formulae, we can see how the Slenderman folklore had such an impact:

1. It refers to a modern phenomenon (a digital ghost), and it relates strongly back to ghost stories and threat coming from the unknown.
2. Slenderman cannot, of itself, harm, and the real danger (in this case physical assault) is driven from the ghost story.
3. Slenderman is easily searchable online but requires effort to build up the discourse around the stories. There it is difficult to grasp readily for those who are not immersed in the folklore, and therefore self-appointed experts are in a position to provide inaccurate information that fills any vacuum.

It is interesting to note that Cohen also refers to 'Seven objects of moral panic', based upon his many years of observation:

1. Young, working-class, violent males
2. School violence, including bullying
3. Drug use
4. Child abuse and paedophilia
5. Sex, violence and the media
6. Welfare cheats
7. Refugees

Clearly, Slenderman has its roots in object 4. However, the fear arising from digital ghost stories can also relate, we would argue, to 2 and 5. The term 'cyberbullying' is now used so frequently, with anything from name calling on social media to the more serious online harassment and abuse, that it has become virtually ubiquitous to any form of online abuse. We return to object 5 when we discuss sexting and the sharing of intimate images in another chapter.

In another example of a concerning (over)reaction from a responsible public body is the *Doki Doki Literature Club*, a 2017 freeware visual novel developed by Team Salvato. This is to all intents and purposes a kind of video game with horror and upsetting story threads. The game is described as an interactive story, that tells a tale of a group of characters who are part of a literature club, one of whom takes her own life. The game introduces significant elements of psychological horror and disturbing themes such as self-harm and suicide. The imagery in the game is fairly innocuous, so the horror comes from the psychology of interactions with characters who are exploring dark themes. There might be a view that this sort of theme should not be presented as a game, in the same way that there is moral opposition to more mainstream crime and violence games such as *Call of Duty* and *Grand Theft Auto*. However, this is perhaps a reflection of a naive view of the complexity of modern video games and how interactive elements present the opportunity for the player to interact with moral complexity. We discussed video games as an artform earlier in the book, and indeed Andy Robertson, a well-known media commentator on gaming, has also called for video games with interactive narrative to be recognised as art, rather than entertainment,[70] drawing parallels with movies and TV shows that present moral ambiguity and social debate.

As we discussed in chapter 2 in relation to children's risk, concerns over the influence of video games have existed for a long time – for almost as long as video games have been available. The 1976 arcade game called *Death Race* was perhaps the first video game to attract this attention. The game, as was typical in 1976, was graphically simple and had a basic, points scoring play style. However, it differed from video game peers such as *Space Invaders* or *Pacman* in that the points scoring scenario was not a sci-fi or fantasy premise but instead, one where points were scored

---

70   www.tedxexeter.com/speakers/andy-robertson-2/

as a result of driving your vehicle over 'gremlins', characters shaped like basic stick men but named as something more fantastic, perhaps to avoid accusations of human slaughter. The game was loosely based around the movie *Death Race 2000*, a science fiction satire where competitors raced across the US gaining competitive advantage and media notoriety by running over pedestrians. The game was criticised in the media and by organisations such as the National Safety Council as being immoral and encouraging violent conduct – the reporting implied that if gamers were playing a game which encouraged the running over of pedestrians, they might be inclined to in real life.[71] At the time this paralleled moral concern about the influence of violence in cartoons on television and film with, particularly, concerns that if children and young people observed violent acts in cartoon form they may act these out in real life. While there has been little evidence of a causation, such concerns still exist in the present day.[72] However, a rigorous academic review of the issue[73] highlighted that evidence does not bear out anecdote or opinion.

However, the keenness to find causation showed no signs of reducing gaming technology and content became increasingly sophisticated. The *Mortal Kombat* series caused controversy and a number of lawsuits upon release in 1992 and was even debated in the US Congress.[74] The advent of the 'first-person shooter' (where one plays the game from the perspective of a gun-wielding protagonist) raised further concerns. One of the first, *Wolfenstein 3D*, was withdrawn from sale in Germany due to allusions to Nazis. However, perhaps one of the most popular original first-person shooters, *Doom*, was supposedly linked to the Columbine massacre and referred to by the offenders.[75]

71   Kocurek, C. A. (2012) 'The agony and the Exidy: A history of video game violence and the legacy of Death Race.' *Game Studies*, 12(1).

72   www.dailymail.co.uk/news/article-1159766/Cartoon-violence-makes-children-aggressive.html

73   Kirsh, S. J. (2006) 'Cartoon violence and aggression in youth.' *Aggression and Violent Behavior*, 11(6): pp. 547-676.

74   https://en.wikipedia.org/wiki/1993_congressional_hearings_on_video_games

75   Frymer, B. (2009) 'The media spectacle of Columbine: Alienated youth as an object of fear.' *American Behavioral Scientist*, 52(10): pp. 1387-1404.

However, if we are to take a critical, objective perspective, we quickly see how these claimed causations bear little scrutiny. The *Doom* and *Doom 2* video games sold approximately two million copies in total[76] and, dating from before downloadable video games and untraceable use, one can assume a far higher number of people played the game in some form through copies and sharing. In the case of the Columbine massacre, post incident it was noted that the two offenders both played *Doom* and also listened to the music of Marilyn Manson, a musician who has sold over 50 million records worldwide. Given the volumes involved in both listening to Marilyn Manson's music, and also playing the *Doom* video game, why would it be a surprise that young people in their teens would be engaging with either?

While it can evidence that, among other video games, they played *Doom*, we cannot evidence that as a result of playing this game, they decided to commit a horrific violent act in a school. If *Doom* was such a causal factor in inciting gun violence, we would have expected to have seen thousands of real-life emulations during the game's prominence. Perhaps, instead, returning once more to Cohen's structure for moral panics, the lack of understanding about the game and our own discomfort with the nature of the content means that subjective opinion takes over, and we look for evidence that does not stand up to scrutiny.

Obviously, the issue of young people accessing violent and/or sexualised content is always going to be of great concern. However, a detailed meta-analysis of research into the influence of video game violence found little in the way of rigorous evidence which justified blaming video games for social ills.[77] The article famously argued that perhaps content-blaming may '*distract society from more pressing concerns such as poverty and education*'.

---

76   Armitage, G. et al. (2006) *Networking and online games: Understanding and engineering multiplayer internet games*. Chichester, England: John Wiley & Sons. p. 14.

77   Ferguson, C. J. (2015) 'Does media violence predict societal violence? It depends on what you look at and when.' *Journal of Communication*, 65(1): pp. E1–E22.

Nevertheless, we still see claimed causations from video games, and this was the case with the *Doki Doki Literature Club*, which was cited by a coroner in the North West of England as being linked to the tragic suicide of Ben Walmsley.[78] As a result of this warning many police forces issued alerts that were sent to schools and, via social media, to parents. It is generally at this point that we are alerted to these announcements, and try, once again, to bring a level of objectivity to the swelling moral panic.

Taking a dispassionate perspective on this case, causation is far more difficult to demonstrate. The *Doki Doki Literature Club* was downloaded over 2 million times.[79] If there was a causal link between playing the game and suicidal ideation, one would expect to see more than one case that refers to it.

The Blue Whale Challenge

Another well-known digital ghost story, that refuses, it seems, to leave the public consciousness is the Blue Whale Challenge, which emerged in 2017 with a modus operandi comprised of an increasingly familiar pattern:

- Public officials in the UK raised concerns about children taking their lives as a result of playing the game, awareness of which had arisen from media reports in overseas locations.

- Social media was used as a channel to 'raise awareness' and bring it into mainstream discourse.

- Media reporting repeated, with uncorroborated figures, the original news articles. In particular with the Blue Whale Challenge, there was media reporting drawn from a local news report about young people taking their own lives in Russia in large numbers.

---

78   The Sun. (2018) *What is the Doki Doki Literature Club and why have schools issued a warning to parents over the DDLC online game?* Available at: www.thesun.co.uk/news/6630711/doki-doki-literature-club-police-school-warning-suicide/ (Accessed: 6 August 2021).

79   PC Games. (2018) *Doki Doki Literature Club! surpasses two million downloads*. Available at: www.pcgamesn.com/doki-doki-literature-club/doki-doki-literature-club-player-numbers (Accessed: 6 August 2021).

For example, the Daily Mail[80] ran the headline:

'Police warn Blue Whale "suicide" Facebook game linked to 130 teen deaths in Russia is heading to the UK.'

While details of the actual operation of the challenge were unclear, it was purported that the challenge involved downloading an app which allegedly gave out 50 different instructions that the recipient would have to enact and report back to the app controller, showing evidence of the acts. These acts included watching scary videos, not speaking to people, or, the activity that led to the name of the challenge, carving a picture of a blue whale into your skin with a razor blade. The 50th instruction was to take your own life.

During 2017, the Blue Whale Challenge was referred to by many with responsibility for child safeguarding (police, education professionals and academics). Perhaps all were coming from a place of concern – wishing to raise alarm to such a harmful game. However, from a poorly checked news story and rapidly shared online images, and no evidence of causation or even verified existence, all they succeeded in doing was raising alarm and alerting young people to this challenge, which we should bear in mind had no evidence of actually existing.

The allegations were given far greater public awareness, and credence, as a result of the sorts of people who commented on social media. These were professionals with safeguarding responsibilities. If they thought this was a concern, surely it must be! Having 'experts' explain what it was gave more credibility to the phenomenon that could, and arguably should, have been easily dismissed as nonsense. However, once the social media shares were expanding, others joined in, again, without checking the original source or accuracy of the reporting. And when social media starts to trend, mainstream media follows, so more news stories emerged warning parents to speak to their children, check their devices, and be on the lookout for evidence of self-harm.

---

80   Daily Mail. (2017) *Police warn Blue Whale 'suicide' Facebook game linked to 130 teen deaths in Russia is heading to the UK.* Available at: www.dailymail.co.uk/news/article-4446556/Police-warn-Blue-Whale-suicide-game-heading-UK.html (Accessed: 6 August 2021).

However, the most concerning thing about the Blue What Challenge was that **it did not exist**. There are still no corroborated cases of self-harm or suicide linked to any tangible 'challenge'. None of the professionals had ever seen the platform or interacted with the app. One would have to assume that if this was something that was downloaded to devices it would be something that one could access and evidence. Or, at the very least, one should be able to share screenshots of the app. There was never any evidence forthcoming. Nevertheless, the digital ghost story remains and continues to be reported on, even in academia. Mukhra et al.,[81] the most widely cited academic paper on the subject, concludes with:

> *'The blue whale challenge, is a deadly online craze. It prompts the victim through online dares ranging from watching a scary movie at midnight, self-harming by making cuts using razors to committing suicides.'*

We reiterate, there is no evidence that the challenge exists.

The fact-checking website *Snopes* also concluded that there was no evidence that the Blue Whale Challenge existed.[82] While there was some evidence of online coercion to self-harm, reported from the widely cited regional Russian media source (that has resulted in at least one prosecution, which, it seems, was the trigger article for all of the mythology around the Blue Whale Challenge) there was no evidence whatsoever regarding this as an organised, app-based, interactive challenge. The folklore around the Blue Whale Challenge is reinforced with research from Cambridge University[83] that has made use of considerable research expertise to conclude no evidence of the existence of the challenge.

---

81   Mukhra, R., Baryah, N., Krishan, K., & Kanchan, T. (2019) '"Blue Whale Challenge": A game or crime?' *Science and engineering ethics*, 25(1): pp. 285-291.

82   Snopes. (2017) *Is the 'blue whale' game responsible for dozens of suicides in Russia?* Available at: www.snopes.com/fact-check/blue-whale-game-suicides-russia/ (Accessed 6 August 2021).

83   Light blue touchpaper. (2019) *Online suicide games: a form of digital self-harm or a myth?* Available at: www.lightbluetouchpaper.org/2019/10/11/online-suicide-games-a-form-of-digital-self-harm-or-a-myth/ (Accessed 6 August 2021).

However, the Blue Whale Challenge refuses to go away. There was a recent spike in media interest once more (for example[84]) claiming it had returned. Upon closer inspection this was as a result of a social media account bearing the name. Post-event, it is no surprise that there are individuals setting up accounts using the name; it is well known now to trigger fear. Equally, there was no evidence that these accounts were doing anything other than copycatting the mythology of the original challenge. Nevertheless, the discovery triggered another round of press releases from police forces and subsequent tabloid media stories. Thus, it continues.

We have spent the first half of this chapter discussing the nature of the digital ghost story and the need for evidence and critical thinking when considering these fables. We now move on to look at another recent ghost story in more depth, and demonstrate, with some fairly compelling evidence, the impact of poor critical thinking on those in our care.

The characteristics of a digital ghost story

A scenario frequently played out in our work goes something like this:

Professional: 'Have you heard of <digital ghost story>? It's causing harm to young people online.'

Weary researcher: 'Really? I haven't seen any evidence of this?'

Professional: 'There are young people in <random nation x> who have died/been harmed as a result.'

Weary researcher: 'How do you know this?'

Professional: 'There was a media story shared on social media.'

Weary researcher: 'So, you haven't actually seen evidence of this yourself?'

Professional: 'No, but <professional organisation y> have put out a press release about it.'

Weary researcher: 'Ah, so they have seen evidence of it?'

---

84   www.mirror.co.uk/news/uk-news/blue-whale-challenge-police-warning-22370203

Professional: 'No, they saw the media story on social media and thought they ought to put out a press release. What do you think we should do to stop <digital ghost story>?'

While it might be slightly tongue-in-cheek to refer to ourselves as 'weary researcher', this is a scenario that has happened many times, and regardless of the moving and changing nature of online safeguarding, beset with new legislation, curriculum demands and insistence on the training of professionals, the concern is always reactive rather than proactive, and driven by online alerts and social media traffic. And while these concerns emerge with the best of intentions, the real impact on young people can be significant and long lasting. We can illustrate that by exploring the Momo Challenge, a ghost story that gained considerable notoriety at the start of 2019.

Momo

The Momo Challenge was publicised by police, press and professionals, and across social media, at the end of February last year.[85] Again, upsetting content was conflated into a ghost story of organised abuse and deaths in far-off lands. We were aware of the 'Momo' image (actually a photograph of a sculpture of an *ubume* – a supernatural entity from Japanese folklore – produced by the artist Keisuke Aisawa[86] in 2016) and its use by trolls, cutting it into child-centric videos on YouTube, in the latter part of 2018. While there were some mentions of it in the popular press in late 2018, these were generally only reported in mainstream tabloid media, and dismissed by most in the safeguarding sector as nothing more than tabloid hysteria. There were certainly no voices of authority commenting at that time and it was not being shared on social media. We took the view that in the same way that the practice of 'Rickrolling'[87] placed a video of the pop star Rick Astley in an unexpected link or video, the Momo Challenge was simply a prank (albeit an unpleasant one) done by trolls and meme creators to generate views and hits on their content and gain some level of notoriety among their peers.

---

85   https://swgfl.org.uk/magazine/digital-ghost-stories/
86   https://instagram.com/p/BlQlfA2Biju/
87   https://en.wikipedia.org/wiki/Rickrolling

In the same way that chain letters[88] prey on the fears of recipients, these memes have a similar goal – while the challenge did not exist, the more people searched for images and videos where the Momo image had been inserted, the more likely it was that young people would be upset seeing it.

The *ubume* image is indeed a shocking one – a face with distorted features and a bird-like body. Clearly the image is disturbing. When we use it in talks to this day, discussing the impact of the Momo challenge, it will generally get groans and people looking away. Bearing in mind that these talks are generally to professionals, and those training to be professionals in the children's workforce, it interesting to note these were the very people directing children and families to search for it due to their response to this particular moral panic (more on this below).

Toward the end of February 2019, Andy received a call from a journalist:

Journalist: 'Have you heard about this Momo thing, it's all over the internet.'

Andy: 'Yes, it's been doing the rounds among the trolls, what's the issue?'

Journalist: 'No it's not, it's getting kids to self-harm.'

Andy: 'A scary image is getting kids to self-harm? How?'

Journalist: 'It waits until parents are asleep then it tells the kids to hurt themselves.'

Andy: 'It?'

Journalist: 'Momo.'

Andy: 'Are you sure? It's just an image injected into videos by trolls.'

Journalist: 'No, it's telling kids to self-harm. There have been deaths in other countries.'

Andy: 'Have there? How do you know?'

Journalist: 'It was reported in local media over there.'

Andy: 'Are there any published coroners' reports?'

---

88   Bennett, C. H., Li, M., and Ma, B. (2003) 'Chain letters & evolutionary histories.' *Scientific American*, 288(60): pp. 76-81.

Journalist: 'Why?'

Andy: 'Ah...'

Upon further investigation, it was clear that the myth had grown considerably from 'trolls place upsetting image in videos to scare children'. The journalist's description was accurate to the myth. The Momo Challenge was an unexplained interactive game – the image would appear in a child-centric video (this is the only factually accurate part of the story). It would know when a parent wasn't in the room, and it would then interact with the child, having a conversation encouraging them to harm themselves. Nevertheless, the stories became more elaborate as the rumours spread across the internet. The media reporting, and associated online folklore, continued to develop. The image would, apparently, speak to the viewer and give them a mobile phone number for them to contact, which would then provide the victim with a series of challenges, allegedly associated with some form of self-harm or instructions to take their life (we can see a lot of parallels with the Blue Whale folklore here). We noticed that while the notoriety grew, the trolling videos started to include 'speech' from Momo (which was either recorded or used software-generated audio). Yet there remained no evidence whatsoever of any interaction coming from these videos. Which is unsurprising, given that this wouldn't have been technically possible!

From 25 February to 2 March 2019, the Momo challenge became big news. During what we have now affectionately named 'Momo week', the UK and US certainly witnessed a moral panic hitting both social and news media, and with social media messaging by professionals and authority figures joining in the panic to give advice and opinion of this (fake) phenomenon. Referred to in the media as an online 'suicide game' that was encouraging children to self-harm and take their own lives, news reports claimed the challenge had been linked to the suicides of children in Argentina, Mexico and India.[89] Obviously, this was very

---

89   The Sun. (2019) *What is the Momo Challenge story, was it the WhatsApp 'suicide game' a hoax and how many deaths has it been linked to?* Available at: www.thesun.co.uk/news/6926762/what-momo-suicide-game-whatsapp-deaths-uk-hoax/ (Accessed: 6 August 2021).

worrying for anyone with children, but until Momo week it was still only attracting the interest of the tabloid media.

During Momo week, what happened diverted us from the chain letter analogy. While chain letters were traditionally propagated at a peer level, the advantage for those wishing to spread a digital ghost story to collect social media presence, likes and notoriety online, is that there are many channels (it would seem) to spread the mythology and raise awareness further. None are better at doing this than an online 'thought leader' – someone with, as a result of either profession or fame, a large online following.

One of the first major triggers for the spike in interest that week came from the Police Service of Northern Ireland (PSNI), who published a press release that raised serious concerns about the potential harm the Momo challenge posed.[90] Some selected highlights of this press release included:

> *'Whilst no official reports have been made to Police, we are aware of the so-called 'Momo' challenge and are already liaising with other UK Police Services to try to identify the extent of the problem and to look for opportunities to deal with this issue.*
>
> *This extremely disturbing challenge conceals itself within other harmless looking games or videos played by children and when downloaded, it asks the user to communicate with 'Momo' via popular messaging applications such as WhatsApp. It is at this point that children are threatened that they will be cursed or their family will be hurt if they do not self-harm.*
>
> *I am disgusted that a so-called game is targeting our young children and I would encourage parents to know what your children are looking at and who they are talking to.'*

In unpicking this press release, it does come across as vaguely ridiculous. It was saying it had seen no examples of Momo acting in the way the

---

90   PSNI. (2019) *PSNI statement regarding Momo Challenge*. Available at: www.psni.police.uk/news/Latest-News/250219-psni-statement-regarding-momo-challenge/ (Accessed: 6 August 2021).

folklore claimed, but this was not going to stop the PSNI describing the claimed activity (for which there was no evidence) and they then doubled down on the concern with inflammatory language about how disgusting this was. This press release was shared many times on social media and through mainstream news channels. As a result, other police forces followed suit with similar announcements. The following was shared with us via professionals with whom we work, as an example of 'online harm alerts' they receive from police:

'Dear Schools and Partners,

As part of our commitment to working in partnership with schools, partners and parents, I am sending this email out expeditiously to ensure you are aware of an internet 'suicide-influencing game' which has come to my attention called The MOMO Challenge which encourages children to harm themselves and is reported to be linked to several deaths around the world and is now appearing across the UK.

Below is a brief summary of what the MOMO Challenge is and we ask that you share this information among your colleague and parent networks.

With no intention to be condescending, given the horrendous nature of the MOMO challenge, I feel it necessary to advise professionals and parents to seriously consider any decision to raise awareness of it to children and young people as a means to safeguard them, unless necessary; as we know, with all good intentions, drawing attention to it may result in them gravitating towards it.

Mirroring the 'Blue Whale' suicide-game of 2017, The MOMO Challenge is targeted at children and young people through social media by people presenting as MOMO, a terrifying looking doll.

The doll encourages them to add a contact on messaging service WhatsApp from an unknown number, once contact is made, children are subsequently bombarded with terrifying images and messages reportedly ranging from threats and dares which encourage them to self-harm and even commit suicide.'

While these releases clearly come from a place of good intentions, can raising awareness, and naming, something of which there is no evidence outside of copy and pasted media reports, deliver on those good intentions? The second one, in particular, does an excellent job of referencing two online ghost stories in the same message. If you're not worried about Momo, you should be worried about the Blue Whale Challenge! Clearly there was no attempt to fact-check any of this information. It was using inflammatory language that would certainly cause concern to those who read it, particularly those who would not fact-check either. And why would they, these releases have come from a reputable source – the police. Coming from sources of authority legitimised the reporting from the more tabloid end of news outlets, and contributed to the growing social media concern from parents, concerned about their children's safety, who then disseminated further.

Another factor in awareness raising that contributed to the moral panic around Momo was the willingness of some self-proclaimed online safety organisations to talk about how to tackle the Momo Challenge (which, we need to bear in mind, didn't exist), and provide resources for schools in how it might be tackled, which were then shared by concerned individuals on social media as well as school and informal education settings (for example, sports clubs). This drove the Momo challenge further into the public consciousness (while still not actually existing). After all, why would these organisations be talking about it, and sharing resources about how to tackle it, if it didn't exist? One such organisation went as far, when challenged on social media, to claim that while they acknowledged the challenge itself might be 'fake news', they have spoken to children and schools who had first-hand experience of it – rather than the more accurate 'We have spoken to schools where children have seen the videos with the image cut into them'.

However, perhaps the most powerful trigger for the massive spike in interest and concern on social media that beset Momo week was something that was perhaps unique at this stage to this particular digital ghost story – celebrity alarm.

According to CBS News[91] on 26 February 2019, Kim Kardashian West (at the time of writing with 164 million followers), shared a screen grab of a post from a follower that started:

'Parents please be aware and very cautious of what your child watches on YouTube and KIDS YOUTUBE. There is a thing called "Momo" that's instructing kids to kill themselves, turn stoves on while everyone is sleep and even threatening to kill the children if they tell their parents. It doesn't come on instantly so it's almost as if it waits for you to leave the room then comes on in mid show.'

Over the top of the screen grab, Ms Kardashian West had added the text '@YouTube, Please help!!' Following this post, and the subsequent media reporting on- and offline, other celebrities, such as UK TV presenter Stacey Solomon, joined in. Ms Solomon subsequently tweeted:

'Okay what the *** is Momo and what have I had to see this horrific thing 22 times in a week. I'm being warned its on @YouTube Kids and @FortniteGame is it? And if it is SORT IT OUT...'[92]

As an aside, and to their credit, at this point YouTube responded in a measured way, not rising to the hysteria:

'Many of you have shared your concerns with us over the past few days about the Momo Challenge-we've been paying close attention to these reports. After much review, we've seen no recent evidence of videos promoting the Momo Challenge on YouTube.'[93]

91 CBS News. (2019) *Kim Kardashian warns parents of 'Momo challenge,' but YouTube says it sees no evidence.* Available at: www.cbsnews.com/ news/kim-kardashian-warns-parents-of-momo-challenge-youtube-take-action/ (Accessed: 6 August 2021).

92 Metro. (2019) *Stacey Solomon terrified of Momo Challenge for her sons' safety after police warning over 'suicide game'.* Available at: https://metro. co.uk/2019/02/27/stacey-solomon-terrified-momo-challenge-sons-safety-police-warning-suicide-game-8762585/ (Accessed: 25 August 2021).

93 ABC Action News. (2019) *Momo Challenge: YouTube says it has seen no recent videos promoting alleged viral challenge.* Available at: www. abcactionnews.com/news/national/momo-challenge-youtube-responds-says-its-seen-no-recent-videos-promoting-alleged-viral-challenge (Accessed: 26 August 2021).

In summary, the timeline that triggered Momo Week ran:

- 25 February 2019: PSNI send press release about their concerns around Momo.
- 26 February 2019: An organisation that sells online safety services to schools posts a 'guide to Momo' to help 'thousands of concerned schools and parents' on social media channels.
- 26 February 2019: Kim Kardashian West posts about Momo on her Instagram page calling for YouTube to help.
- 27 February 2019: Other celebrities start commenting regarding their concerns about Momo on social media.

As a result, social media exploded with concern from parents which, over time, lead to increasingly bizarre claims about the Momo Challenge. Claims included:

- Someone's son was 'targeted' by Momo last year in Spain
- Someone has a 6-year-old who is terrified to leave her bed because of Momo
- Someone's 7-year-old knows someone who walked in front of a car because they were told to by Momo
- Someone calling for their children's primary school to speak to the pupils about Momo
- Someone claiming that their children's school have already done classes on Momo.

Thankfully, toward the end of Momo Week there was more responsible media reporting,[94] measured social media voices and communication by many safeguarding professionals and academics (ourselves included) that caused the panic to die down and interest in Momo waned.

We conducted follow-up work across the sector to examine what impact this particularly problematic response to a ghost story had caused. We acknowledge that most people engaged in the moral panic from Momo did not do so because they wished to cause harm, but because they

---

94 www.theguardian.com/technology/2019/feb/28/viral-momo-challenge-is-a-malicious-hoax-say-charities

believed it was the responsible thing to do, with children's wellbeing at the heart of their actions. However, these behaviours had a potentially very negative impact on the very children they wanted to protect.

Google Trends, a tool provided by Google that gives relative popularity of search terms against all others over a given time period, is useful here. It allows us to see the search terms that are most popular. Essentially a search term is given a value between 0 (not searched for much at all) and 100 (searched for a lot). Searches on Google for 'Momo challenge' in the UK in the weeks before, during and after Momo week were:

17/02/2019: 5

24/02/2019: 100

03/03/2019: 13

Clearly, there had been an awful lot of searches for Momo that week.

A source of evidence closer to schools themselves was drawn from search data carried out in school settings. As a result of our relationships with providers in the sector, we were able to access search data from 2681 schools. In contrast to Google Trends, the data we received involved specific numbers of searches. Due to the way in which the data were collected (through monitored devices used by pupils) we are confident these are searches carried out by children, rather than by members of staff. If we consider each day of Momo week:

25/02/2019: 453 searches for Momo-related terms

26/02/2019: 1332 searches for Momo-related terms

27/02/2019: 5944 searches for Momo-related terms

28/02/2019: 15,371 searches for Momo-related terms

29/02/2019: 11,364 searches for Momo-related terms

In the whole week before, there were 76 searches for Momo-related terms. So, as a percentage, as a result of a great deal of publicity and knee-jerk reaction, the schools in our sample saw a 45,000% increase in searches for Momo during Momo week.

As a further indicator of impact, we can draw on a survey with young people. This is a survey with schools (www.surveymonkey.co.uk/r/ypinternet), in partnership the online safety charity SWGfL (www.swgfl.org.uk/) that we have run with schools over the last five years. The survey asks general questions of young people about their use of digital technology, their concerns, and any upsetting encounters they have experienced. There are now over 13,000 responses to the survey, which provides us with a robust data set. The question that is of interest to this exploration of the impact of Momo week is:

• Question 9 'If you have been upset by something you've seen online, would you like to explain what this was?'[95]

By exploring the responses to question 9 we can determine whether Momo was something that young people disclose as something they have seen as upsetting.

In drawing from the survey responses, we can divide between those collected before Momo Week and those immediately after. For the period of time prior to Momo week (from 1 January 2016 to 24 February 2019), there were:

• 9525 responses to the survey with 0 mentions of Momo by young people disclosing things they had seen they had been upset by online.

From the year immediately after Momo week (1 March 2019 to 1 March 2020) there were:

• 741 responses to the survey with 41 mentions of Momo by young people disclosing things they had seen they had been upset by online.

All of the young people who disclosed Momo as something upsetting they had seen online were of primary school age. Furthermore, at the time of writing (over a year and a half since Momo week), we still see it rear its head among young people. A response to the same question this week was 'There was someone called Momo on *Among Us*, and

---

95 This follows the question 'Have you ever seen anything upsetting online?'

he told me to kill myself'.[96] Clearly, Momo is still lurking as a myth online.

Responding to digital ghost stories

We have, in this chapter, been somewhat critical of the well-meaning but poorly considered response of someone who is responding to a natural instinct to protect children from harm. We argue strongly for a far greater level of critical thinking when it comes to responding to online safeguarding concerns, particularly those ghost stories that have a mythology preceding them, becoming increasingly embellished with every social media share.

It is important to pause when these things surface. Rather than believing something at face value, take some time to reflect and maybe do some fact-checking. The challenge is that, in some cases, the stories might not always be nonsense. Not long after contact from a local college regarding the 'resurgence of the Blue Whale Challenge', which was quickly dismissed as a hoax, Andy was contacted again about rumours of a 'suicide video' on TikTok. Again, this had come from a police alert, and the college felt it showed all the hallmarks of another ghost story. However, in this case it was true. As was reported by TikTok,[97] this was a recording of a live-stream from Facebook, where a US citizen – Ronnie McNutt – had taken his own life. This video clip was cut into other videos (similar to the cutting of Momo images into videos), and from what TikTok described as a co-ordinated attack on their platform, these videos were uploaded from multiple accounts onto their platform. The police advice in this case went on to say that they would recommend no pupils use any TikTok films from three 24-hour periods, and that they should be warned about the suicide videos.

---

96   To clarify this point, *Among Us* is a multiplayer game – a kind of *Cluedo* in space. Players interact to solve the 'whodunnit' mystery on board a space craft. The game had clearly not been infiltrated by Momo, however, someone had created an account called Momo, and was using the same phrases from the Momo myth to scare other players.

97   www.theguardian.com/technology/2020/sep/22/dark-web-responsible-for-tiktok-suicide-video-says-company

We would disagree. In cases of ghost stories, as well as those that are more real, we would deliver a similar message – young people cannot be protected from every single piece of harmful content or conduct online. While TikTok, to their credit, were extremely proactive in taking down these videos and blocking accounts uploading it, they were, for a time, available on the platform. We also know, from our many hours speaking to young people about these sorts of issues, that they are concerned that, if they do disclose that they have seen something upsetting, or engaged in harmful discourse, their devices will be monitored or removed. We would, therefore, suggest a simple and direct approach. Young people should not be alerted to every ghost story, or real example of harmful content, that the online world throws up. However, it can be explained to them that there might be times when they are online and something happens that they find upsetting. In those cases, they should be encouraged to speak to someone about it. If they are able, they could record a screen grab of what they have seen, as it will help them explain what has happened, and help adults support them.

We have explored many ghost stories in this chapter, and we have shown through an exploration of Momo week how the best of intentions can result in driving young people to the thing from which we are trying to protect them. There will be more ghost stories and more examples of harmful content. Young people need to know they can say when they're upset and that there are things that can be done to help. Once again, good digital parenting all comes down to the quality of the conversation between children and adults.

Chapter 4
Teen sexting – the modern-day phenomenon

In this chapter we consider the 'modern-day phenomenon' of sexting – the sending and receiving of intimate images using digital technology, with a particular focus on what is referred to by some as 'teen sexting'. We will focus on the exchange of images in heterosexual relationships. This is not because sexting is absent from the lives of LGBT+ young people as well, but we focus on heterosexual relationships here because this is where the majority of our data comes from, and therefore this is where we feel best qualified to hold a view. However, this is not to say that image-based abuse is not also an issue within LGBT+ relationships – our discussions with the Revenge Porn Helpline,[98] a service for adult victims of image-based abuse, estimate about 20-25% of their victims come from LGBT+ relationships.

The term 'sexting' refers to the self-generation and distribution of intimate images to either one or more recipients. It is viewed as a phenomenon of the digital age and consequently attracts much media interest (for example[99]). The word itself was a media creation, a conflation of 'sexual texting' which drew in the sharing of self-generated images, something that has become extremely straightforward to do with mobile technology since the early 2000s. Celebrities brought the behaviour to the attention of the media[100] who set about blending 'sex' and 'texting' into

---

98 www.revengepornhelpline.org.uk/
99 www.dailymail.co.uk/news/article-2246154/Sex-texts-epidemic-Experts-warn-sharing-explicit-photos-corrupting-children.html
100 www.theatlantic.com/national/archive/2011/06/brief-history-sexting/351598/

the 'sexting' form. Since this point, sexting has become well established in the modern technology lexicon.

Over time more media attention was drawn from this practice being carried about by teenagers – unsurprising perhaps, given the need for headlines not only to sell physical newspapers but also generate page views online that can be converted into advertising revenue. As is typical of the media, particularly in its more tabloid products, the focus was always on those that resulted in the most serious impacts, in order to garner media attention. One of the highest profile stories related to Jesse Logan, who took her own life following a prolonged period of abuse that resulted from her sending a nude image to her boyfriend, who then chose to share it to peers.[101]

Another extremely high-profile case that attracted much media attention was Amanda Todd, who engaged in a sexting related incident with a stranger on a webcam, which resulted in further coercion by the abuser and then abuse by peers once the abuser released the images online.[102]

Teen sexting, as it has unhelpfully been referred to over the years, is something we, and Andy in particular, have been involved in researching for many years. What becomes apparent when exploring these issues with young people, is its mundanity in their eyes, and alarm that such behaviour can result in the harms described in cases such as Jesse Logan and Amanda Todd.

A brief history of teen sexting research

At the start of this research, back in 2008, there were many questions around 'Why do teens do this?' and 'Why would they place themselves at risk?' As with a lot of our research, we are generally exploring the fallout and harm that arises from when sexting 'goes wrong' – a typical scenario being a teen taking an image on their mobile device and either sending as a result of a request, or sending unsolicited, to an either willing or unsuspecting recipient. As we were told by teens, in most cases this is where the activity ends. Images are exchanged, boundaries

101 www.huffpost.com/entry/jessica-logan-suicide-par_n_382825
102 https://en.wikipedia.org/wiki/Suicide_of_Amanda_Todd

are respected, images are not retained when a relationship breaks down. However, in some cases, the images are forwarded, non-consensually, to other recipients. This tends to be where the harm that can arise from these behaviours starts – the victim of the sharing might be abused and mocked and the images may resurface again and again.

The catalyst for research into these behaviours was that schools were increasingly disclosing that they were dealing with incidents where a self-produced image has ended up in the hands of more than the intended recipient, and as a result there was some fallout abuse happening. They, essentially, had to deal with the times a sexting incident resulted in an image being shared and then disclosed to a teacher. And many did not know how to go about this.

We will, throughout this chapter, return to the legalities around sexting and it is, by the letter of the law, illegal. The 1978 Protection of Children Act (section one) makes it clear that the production or distribution of an indecent image of a minor is illegal. However, as is clear from the year of the act, the development of the legislation took place in a time when it was not conceived that the taker of the image might also be the subject of the image, and that the subject was a minor. As we will explore in more detail, this law was introduced to prevent the exploitation of minors by adults in the manufacture of 'child pornography',[103] not to criminalise those engaging in exactly the same behaviour as adults in relationships. Nevertheless, it was made very clear, in the early emergence of teen sexting, that what the victim of the abuse had done was illegal and they could be charged. It was generally acknowledged in schools at the time that there was no guidance – teachers didn't know whether confiscating a device with the image would result in them being in possession of indecent images of a minor, and whether they should call the police.

However, when this was raised at a national level – the problems of dealing with teen sexting or, more correctly, dealing with teen sexting where images had been shared non-consensually and someone was being abused as a result – it was frequently dismissed. It would seem that, at the

---

103 This is an unhelpful and still used phrase to describe the production of child abuse material. Pornography implies consent and sexual excitement, neither of which are part of the production of this sort of imagery.

time, society was not prepared to face the fact that teens were using their mobile phones in the same way many adults were.

Therefore, we decided to work with young people to try to determine the scale of the issues, and whether it was something that required more effective intervention and support. In the very first conversation Andy had with a group of teens about this 'modern-day phenomenon'[104] and whether this was something that was experienced by their peers, he looked at a room of blank faces whom he had told:

'We want to do some research into sexting.'

'What's that?' came the responses from the young people in the room.

'When people take intimate images of themselves on their mobiles and send the images to other people. Then sometimes people send them to other people without the permission of the original sender.'

'Oh yeah, that happens all the time. Why do you call it sexting?'

We have been told many times over the years that 'sexting' is a term used by 'old people' – young people are more likely to use terms such as 'dick pics', 'tit pics', 'pussy pics' or simply 'nudes'. Nevertheless, even in the early days of this research, young people took the view that this was something that happened among peers and they would end up seeing images, even if they had not asked to see them, as they would be shared among peers on group chats and similar. While some young people had concerns about the non-consensual sharing of these images, the focus of blame frequently lay, in their view, with the originator of that image. To paraphrase, a frequent opinion expressed was:

'If they don't want it shared, don't send it in the first place.'

When asked questions about attitudes toward the person who would choose to non-consensually share the image further, many would express

---

104 It is with some amusement we often hear this being referred to as a modern-day phenomenon given that the sale of Polaroid cameras in the 70s were, arguably, driven as a result of the wish to produce intimate images at home without the embarrassment of taking the film to the local camera shop for development.

opinions that while this was not really acceptable, it was really down to the originator of the image to take responsibility.

However, one thing that did arise frequently was that fallout and abuse resulting from sexting incidents would rarely involve resolution with the help of adults. When asked what adults can do to help, the frequent comments were:

'Listen, don't judge, and understand.'

However, it was the view of young people that in reality, most adults would lose their minds, tell off the victim of abuse, or demand involvement of the police because a crime had been committed. There was a clear view of young people, even in these early discussions, that adults just didn't get it, and would aim to prevent sexting through scary messages of ending up with a criminal record, or simply 'Don't do it otherwise you've only got yourselves to blame when things go wrong'.

Speaking to adults, whether these be teachers, parents or policy makers, the young people's views were often confirmed. It was never a case of 'How do we support young people who become victims of abuse as a result of non-consensual sharing?' It was instead the more prohibitive 'How do we stop them doing this?', 'No way would any children here do this' or, even better, 'Isn't there a piece of technology that can stop them from doing this?'

The belief that 'our children wouldn't do this', from both an institutional and parental perspective, is an interesting one, in that it frames the act of exchanging images as something that will only impact on those directly involved. We have, throughout this book, discussed our own experiences in discussions with young people and adults about youth digital behaviours. In one instance Andy visited a school to deliver an assembly and workshops with Year 8 pupils around digital behaviours. While the focus of the talk and discussions was not sexting, this was mentioned – more in the context of 'There might be times when someone asks you to do something online you're uncomfortable with, it's OK to say no' and 'The way to start a relationship with someone is not to send nudes'. The subject matter was checked with the school first, as is always the case, and they acknowledged that they had dealt with a couple of instances of sexting in this year group, so they felt it entirely relevant.

While the assembly and workshops were well received by both pupils and staff, a parent took exception to the subject matter and complained to the head and chair of governors. While we won't share a copy of the full text of the complaint here, the central gist of the concern was that 'Children who do this should be spoken to separately' and 'My daughters would never do this, so they don't need to know about it'. The parent seemed to be of the view that because her daughters would not engage in such practices themselves, there was no need to make them aware of the context, or the fact that if these sorts of things do happen, they should speak to a teacher about it.

The belief that 'If you will talk about it they will do it more' is a common trope in this area, and one that is not borne out in reality. The fact of the matter is that young people learn about these behaviours, and form beliefs around their acceptability, from peers, unless there is an educational intervention. There is no evidence to show that having lessons about sexting encourages practice and, furthermore, young people regularly express their wish to be able to ask questions around these more sensitive topics and to get answers to them. We might suggest, given our experiences in this area for quite a while, that these beliefs come more from an unwillingness by the adult to have what might be an awkward conversation with a young person, rather than valid concern around encouragement of practice.

Returning to the mother's concerns, perhaps a way of illustrating the naivety of this view comes from a news story in 2018, where, in Denmark, approximately 1000 adolescents were charged with the distribution of indecent imagery of minors.[105] The story centred on the sharing of two video clips of two 15-year-olds engaged in a sexual act. Facebook alerted Danish police to the sharing of the video, and shared details of those who had shared, and received, the videos on their Messenger platform. Those who had shared and received the videos, it was reported in other news sources, ranged in age from 14 to 25.[106] While the legal issues around this

---

105 BBC. (2018) *Denmark Facebook sex video: More than 1000 young people charged.* Available at: www.bbc.co.uk/news/world-europe-42694218 (Accessed: 10 August 2021).

106 The New York Times. (2018) *1000 Danes accused of child pornography for sharing videos of teens.* Available at: www.nytimes.com/2018/01/15/world/europe/denmark-child-pornography-video.html (Accessed: 10 August 2021).

case are something we will return to later in the chapter, it is a useful illustration now to show how quickly this sort of content can be spread but also how it can be sent without the consent of the recipient. Many of the young people charged in this case claimed they had been sent the videos without asking for them, and had not shared them further. Nevertheless, they were still under investigation as a result of receiving them.

To return to the mother's concern, it is perfectly possible that her daughters would not engage in the production and exchange of intimate images themselves. In much of the work we have done around this practice, young people are generally of the view that it isn't something that many of their peers are doing. However, due to the sharing of images, they get exposed to the sharing of them, and indeed this has been discussed in a recent Ofsted report.[107] Or, to put it more succinctly, as a result of discussing this parental concern with a subsequent group of young people, one young man suggested:

'Yeah, they might not do it, but that doesn't stop them receiving a pic of someone's dick.'

A little blunt, perhaps, but very much cognisant of the wider context in which sexting practices are not simply about the behaviours of those involved in the original exchange of images. As has been raised in other research,[108 109] this is 'normal' for a lot of teens – while they may not, of themselves, engage in it, they are aware of it going on and of its impact.

We would argue that in order to better understand teen sexting, and therefore better support young people who get abused, we need to step

107 www.gov.uk/government/publications/review-of-sexual-abuse-in-schools-and-colleges

108 Ringrose, J., Gill, R., Livingstone, S., and Harvey, L. (2012) *A qualitative study of children, young people and 'sexting': A report prepared for the NSPCC*. London: National Society for the Prevention of Cruelty to Children.

109 Phippen, A. (2012) *Sexting: An exploration of practices, attitudes and influences*. Available at: www.blackpoolsafeguarding.org.uk/assets/uploads/resources/For%20Professionals/Sexting%20-%20An%20Exploration%20of%20Practices,%20Attitudes%20and%20Influences.pdf (Accessed: 9 August 2021).

back and better understand the social and biological content of these behaviours. As mentioned in the footnote above, sexting is a digital manifestation of an analogue behaviour. Put simply, this is now part of the courtship ritual. We have had many conversations with adults who engage in such practices, and we understand that the unsolicited dick pic is now a common part of interaction on online data platforms such as Tinder. Adolescents are growing into adults; sexual awakening and the wish for relationships are all part of this development. With a death of effective relationships and sex education in schools, rather than posing the question 'Why are teens engaging in sexting?', perhaps a better question would be 'Why wouldn't teens engage in sexting?' Something that has become a standard within the adult courtship ritual in the digital age is bound to bleed down into adolescence, and without effective education around potential risks, emergent harms, and the very fundamental aspects of relationship development such as consent, boundaries and respect, it is little wonder young people will sometimes emulate adult behaviours.

A conversation that Andy once had with a young man as part of a group discussion has gained somewhat folklore-like notoriety in the online safeguarding community, but illustrates this point perfectly:

Interviewer: 'Why do boys send dick pics?'

Young man: 'To get a nude back.'

Interviewer: 'Does this ever work?'

Young man: 'No, never.'

Within this snatch of dialogue from a wider discussion, there is an illustration of the adolescent mindset – this is the sort of thing you do if you want a relationship and if you persevere, you might end up exchanging images with a partner. When subsequently asked why keep doing it if this never results in the hoped outcome, the young man simply said:

'Well, one day it might.'

The triumph of hope over experience clearly prevailed.

It would be wonderful to be able to report that, as a result of over ten years' research, and to a certain extent, lobbying, around teen sexting, we could move the discussion on to say that from these early discussions, more recent chats with young people resulted in them being knowledgeable about the risks associated with the exchange of intimate images with a clear view of who is to blame, and who needs to be punished, in the event of a non-consensual sharing of imagery, and young people confident in the knowledge that if they do become a victim of abuse as a result of these practices, there are adults they can turn to who can help and focus on supporting the victim. We would love to be able to say that the media narrative has moved on from outrage at the moral depravity of these delinquent youngsters (who are simply replicating the acts of adults in relationships), that policy makers are developing progressive thinking to change legislation that protects rather than prosecutes victims, and that schools have curriculum that allows young people to explore issues around the formation of relationships and to be able ask questions in a safe and supportive environment.

However, sadly this is not the case. At the time of writing, an All-Party Parliamentary Group in Westminster has set up an inquiry with the question *'"Selfie Generation": What's behind the rise of self-generated indecent images of children online?'* It would seem that those with a responsibility for the safeguarding of minors are still chasing their tails asking the same questions and with little willingness to move the discourse on from moral outrage that young people might do such a thing. How refreshing it would be to see a call for evidence that perhaps instead said, 'How do we support young people who are the victims of the non-consensual sharing of intimate imagery?'

Tackling sexting in 2021

Society seems unable to ask these more progressive questions because we're not yet ready to accept a complex narrative of sexual agency and growing up on a digital, public stage. Returning to Cohen's reflections on moral panics,[110] he details seven 'objects of normal moral panic'. One of these, object 4, is 'Child Abuse, Satanic Rituals and Paedophile Registers'.

---

110 Cohen, S. (2011) *Folk devils and moral panics*. New York: Routledge.

He describes this as:

> '*The familiar criminal triangle – child (innocent victim); adult (evil perpetrator) and bystanders (shocked but passive).*'

In order for us to be able to be seen to help, we need the child to be a victim to a knowing and evil abuser. The media narrative needs to position the child as the victim and the adult as the abuser, otherwise it loses impact.[111] And the political will follows the media narrative. A more complex account of a teen who sends an image to someone in one scenario, then choses to share an image of another peer they have received from someone else in another, certainly does not fit this simple narrative.

The barriers to a more progressive perspective on sexting among adolescents were perfectly illustrated in a recent piece of media reporting. In January 2021, the Internet Watch Foundation,[112] the excellent organisation whose mission is to 'eliminate child sexual abuse imagery online', put out a press release announcing new research[113] that showed:

> '*Predatory online groomers are a "grave and widespread threat" to children in their bedrooms as new figures reveal the record-breaking scale of child sexual abuse imagery on the internet.*'

There is much to draw from this press release, from both the stakeholder perspective on teen sexting but also, given our focus throughout this book on the need for critical thinking when considering online issues faced by young people and the need to avoid knee-jerk reactions to what

---

111 It is interesting to note that Cohen does refer to peer-on-peer bulling within these objects of normal moral panic, but in this case the bullying relates to violence, and the wider panic about school shootings in the US, rather than bullying that might result from the sharing of intimate images of peers. It certainly would not fit in with a scenario of adolescents placing themselves at risk as a result of wishing to engage in sexual discourse with a peer that resulted in fallout, upset and subsequent abuse.

112 http://www.iwf.org.uk/

113 Internet Watch Foundation. (2021) '*Grave threat' to children from predatory internet groomers as online child sexual abuse material soars to record levels*. Available at: www.iwf.org.uk/news/%E2%80%98grave-threat%E2%80%99-to-children-from-predatory-internet-groomers-as-online-child-sexual-abuse (Accessed: 9 August 2021).

is presented, we can see that when one begins to unpick the rhetoric it can be somewhat problematic.

The press release continued:

'A record number of reports of online child sexual abuse have been processed by the UK's Internet Watch Foundation (IWF).

The IWF, the UK charity responsible for finding and removing images and videos of child sexual abuse from the internet, has also seen a dramatic 77% increase in the amount of "self-generated" abuse material as more children, and more criminals, spend longer online in 2020.'

Clearly, the headline is alarming and worrying to any parent, particularly during a lockdown where children might be in their bedrooms doing schoolwork or interacting with friends they cannot see in person. A headline like this very clearly states that children are more at risk during a lockdown when they are spending far more social and school time online. It would seem like a perfectly reasonable reaction that a parent might decide to ask their child to only be online in family spaces or even imposing some level of monitoring on internet access, in order to be reassured their children are safe when engaging with this increasingly hostile online world (as we discuss in chapter 5).

The facts presented show, on first glance at least, that this is a growing problem:

'In 2020, IWF analysts processed 299,600 reports, which include tip offs from members of the public. This is up from 260,400 reports in 2019. This is an increase of 15%.

Of these reports, 153,350 were confirmed as containing images and/or videos of children being sexually abused. This compares to 132,700 in 2019 – an increase of 16%. Every report contains between one, and thousands of child sexual abuse images and videos. This equates to millions of images and videos.

Of these, 68,000 reports were tagged as including "self-generated" child sexual abuse content – a 77% increase on 2019's total of 38,400 reports.'

However, upon further inspection is this really the case? As a result of reports received, IWF analysts have processed (i.e. visited an online location to examine whether it provides access to child abuse imagery) 15% more reports than in the previous year. It is not clear from the report whether they have deployed more analysts to do this, or whether the same number of analysts have been busier. However, as a result of visiting 15% more online spaces where it has been disclosed they might contain child abuse imagery, they have discovered 16% more imagery than in the previous year. Would this not be the case if one searches in more places that it has been disclosed that people have seen child abuse imagery?

However, perhaps most concerning, particularly in the context of this chapter, is the claim that there has been a significant increase in the type of content that has been classified as self-generated.[114] So the narrative in this press release conflates the sharing of self-produced images among peers with those obtained through coercion by adult groomers. Further exploration of the press release elaborates on the self-generated nature of a lot of these images [bold has been added by us for emphasis]:

> 'Self-generated content can include child sexual abuse content which has been created using webcams, very often in the child's own room, and then shared online.
>
> In **some** cases, children are groomed, deceived or extorted into producing and sharing a sexual image or video of themselves.
>
> **Some** of these videos contain Category A material – the most severe level of abuse which includes penetrative sexual activity.'

This is where the rhetoric becomes more concerning. The press release is firstly conflating child sexual abuse imagery where an adult would abuse a child, with that self-produced by a minor. There is also a certain vagueness where it is suggested that there is a strong link between self-produced imagery and child grooming (the use of the word 'some' provides little measurable comparison of the proportion that would have

---

114 While we will, during this chapter, refer to self-generated, self-produced or youth-produced imagery, because these are the terms used in education, policy and media discussions, we would rather this was not the case. All of these terms imply voluntary production.

been coerced, rather than voluntarily produced and shared, in the first instance, by the young person in the image). The intention of the message is clear – young people are at risk of grooming during lockdown and they are being encouraged to take images of themselves by groomers.

The press release concluded with a quote from the Home Office Minister with a responsibility for child safeguarding:

'**Home Office Minister Victoria Atkins** *said parents need to be supported in starting conversations with their children to help them identify signs of coercion and abuse.*

Ms Atkins said: "The rise in self-generated indecent images of children is deeply concerning. Posting and sharing such images poses psychological harm to children, including feelings of distress and embarrassment... I am delighted that Home Office funding is being used to support the development of the IWF's campaign to tackle youth-produced sexual imagery... This campaign will support parents in starting conversations with their children around keeping safe online and empowers young people to identify the signs of coercion and report abuse."'

The conflation of the self-produced image with that which has been coerced from a minor by an abusive adult feeds into our discussions around moral panics but also shows why the narrative, and support for young people, has not moved on. While the organisation is quite rightly raising awareness of the fact that some self-produced images end up in the hard drives of those with a sexual interest in children, much does not. The press release implies that, during lockdown, many young people will be placing themselves at risk of abuse by predators as a result of engaging in the self-generation of intimate images and they evidence this with statistics that show more analysis elicits more discoveries of illegal imagery. There is encouragement to 'check-up' on children in their bedrooms, and there is clear alignment with Cohen's 'object 4'. We must maintain a state of moral panic around adolescents self-producing intimate images and sharing them, emulating adult behaviour, rather than appreciating problems with the law and a need to support young people who become victims of the non-consensual sharing of these images.

To reiterate – early research, back in 2008/09, had young people calling for adults to 'Listen, don't judge, and understand'. They are still calling for this, while we wring our hands and ask asinine questions such as 'How can we put a stop to this?' And this, we are afraid, is failing young people who have been asking for help for a very long time.

Law fit for the hyperconnected world?

Let us consider two scenarios (we apply them to heterosexual male/female relationships here, but they could be applied to any kind).

In the first one an 18-year-old female takes an intimate image of herself and sends it to her boyfriend; they have been together for nine months. Unfortunately, the relationship breaks down and the now ex-boyfriend decides to send the image to some of his friends, which he justifies as 'revenge' for her ending the relationship. She is made aware of this image being shared, contacts the police and the ex-boyfriend is arrested and charged with the non-consensual sharing of an intimate image under section 33 of the Criminal Justice and Courts Act 2015.

In the second scenario a 17-year-old female takes an intimate image of herself and sends it to her boyfriend; they have been together for nine months. Unfortunately, the relationship breaks down and the now ex-boyfriend decides to send the image to some of his friends, which he justifies as 'revenge' for her ending the relationship. She is made aware of this image being shared, and contacts the police who arrest him for the manufacture and production of an indecent image of a minor under section one of the Protection of Children Act 1978. They also potentially arrest her under the same legislation (although this is increasingly less likely as police become more experienced at handling such situations).

As we have already discussed, this was a piece of legislation being applied to scenarios for which it was never intended. It could not have been in the minds of the legislators that the subject of the image, the taker of the image, and the distributor of the image, could all be the same person. Indeed, if we explore a little bit of history, we can see that the motivation for the legislation arose from a 1970s obscenity campaigner,

Mary Whitehouse,[115] whose lobbying around concerns that children were being exploited and harmed in the production of pornography by adults resulted in a Private Member's Bill by the Bexleyheath Member of Parliament Cyril Townsend. This was clearly understood at the time, and Mr Townsend's obituary by former MP Tam Dalyell,[116] specifically states:

> *'He was prescient in his worries about child pornography and the sexual exploitation of children and in 1978 secured the passage into law of a private member's bill on the Protection of Children.'*

If one digs around Hansard[117] [118] to review the debate around the development of the bill, it is clear that the focus was on the protection of children from exploitation by *adult* pornographers.

The nature of all of the debate around the bill was that children required legislation to ensure they were not exploited by adults wishing to exploit them for sexual and financial gain. This is the sole motivation for the introduction of this legislation, and it was effective up to the point that technology was developed such that a minor could self-produce images.

As we have already explored in this chapter, we now have a legislative tension between on the one hand protecting the victim, and on the other hand addressing the illegality of the generation and sharing. Yet we have to ask ourselves whether a minor who chooses to self-produce an image and send it to another minor is a victim of exploitation or one being abused in the production of pornography? This is where the law falls down completely. There are clearly some incidents where there might be coercion or threat in the minor making the image or video of themselves,

---

115 Thompson, B. (2012) *Ban this filth!: Letters from the Mary Whitehouse Archive*. London: Faber and Faber.

116 Tam Dalyell. (2013) *Obituary – Sir Cyril Townsend: Member of Parliament*. Available at: www.independent.co.uk/news/obituaries/sir-cyril-townsend-member-of-parliament-8974043.html (Accessed 9 August 2021).

117 Hansard is the verbatim recording of debates in Parliament: https://hansard.parliament.uk/

118 Phippen, A., and Brennan, M. (2020) *Sexting and revenge pornography: Legislative and Social dimensions of a modern digital phenomenon*. New York: Routledge.

and there are certainly lots of cases where a self-produced image is shared non-consensually by one minor to another. However, by the letter of the law, all of these people (the producer, the non-consensual sharer and the adult coercer) should all be treated, and punished, equally. There have been many cases that have resulted in minors ending up with criminal records for engaging in these practices.

This has, since these cases started to come into the public eye, resulted in some conflict within some cases. Criminal prosecution in the UK appears to conflict with the views of leading police officers[119] regarding how the law should intervene on issues of sexting/revenge porn among minors. The National Police Chiefs' Council (NPCC) advice seemed to take a more pragmatic view. This more pragmatic view argues that a producer in a sexting case, while technically breaking the laws around distribution of indecent images, is someone that is unlikely to represent a particular threat to anybody in general. Therefore, this fails a 'public interest' check[120] when a decision to prosecute is being made. This applies particularly when it could be argued that the offender is as much a victim as the criminal. This perspective is backed up by the UK's Crown Prosecution Service (CPS).[121] Both CPS and police chief advice go on to suggest that those who will take images from others and redistribute them, and do this repeatedly, should be tackled with the laws that are available to address their behaviour.

The law can be applied in a sensible manner in some cases. In February 2015, two teenage boys, aged 14 and 15 at the time of the offences, were charged in relation to the possession and distribution of indecent photographs of children after one boy had sold the other photographs

---

119 www.npcc.police.uk/ThePoliceChiefsBlog/
SextingyoungpeopleandthepoliceWorkingtowardsacommo.aspx
120 The Crown Prosecution Service has a 'Full Code Test' which is used to make decisions on whether to move to prosecution. The first phase is the 'Evidence Test' – judging if there is sufficient evidence to prosecute – and the second is the 'Public Interest Test' – judging whether it is in the public interest to move to prosecute. www.cps.gov.uk/publications/code_for_crown_prosecutors/codetest.html
121 www.cps.gov.uk/legal/a_to_c/communications_sent_via_social_media/

sent to him by his ex-girlfriend, who was under 16 at the time.[122] Successful prosecution resulted in both offenders being given referral orders. This appeared to be a reasonable and pragmatic application of the law, following CPS advice and looking to punish the abusers, not the victim. However, this was not reflected in some of the public reaction to the case. One of the comments left in response to the reporting of the case (by a female poster on a Facebook page belonging to a local newspaper) seemed to gain great support from fellow posters:

> *'She sent the pictures in the first place, why hasn't she been charged with distributing images? He wouldn't have had any to sell if she hadn't sent them ... She started it all the minute she pressed "send" on that selfie.'*

However, we would strongly argue against this. While the victim did voluntarily take intimate images of herself and share them with her, then, boyfriend, at no point did she consent to them being shared further. The implication that you consent to sharing as soon as you press send is simply nonsense – an offline parallel might be if one has consented to sexual activity with a partner on one occasion, one consents to any further activity with the same partner. Given the tendency of schools to deliver what we might term 'sexting education' as little more than the statement 'Don't do it, it's illegal', the young man who chose to sell these images to his friend would have likely been in little doubt that what he was doing was wrong. However, he chose freely to do so and as a result was guilty of profiting from indecent images of a minor. We have little objection to the application of the law in this case, but we worry about the victim-centric blame that arose.

In our work in schools we have heard on many occasions that someone who distributed to further third parties was not being malicious and was perhaps only doing it 'for a laugh'. Even in our early work in this area[123] it was highlighted that while further distribution was not unusual, most

---

122 Agate, J., and Phippen, A. (2015) 'New social media offences under the Criminal Justice and Courts Act and Serious Crime Bill: the cultural context.' *Entertainment Law Review*, 26(3): pp. 82-87.

123 Phippen, A. (2009) *Sharing personal images and videos among young people*. South West Grid for Learning & University of Plymouth.

young people surveyed did not think this was done for malicious reasons. In our experience, a number of times the fault of redistribution was viewed as clearly lying with the victim, who 'shouldn't have sent it out in the first place if they didn't want it to go further'.

Outcome 21 – The legal sticking plaster

In the growing body of research, and public discomfort, around the criminalisation of minors for engaging in sexting activity, in 2016 the College of Policing[124] issued its own guidance, which allows a sexting incident to be reported and recorded, without the child ending up with a criminal record. This allowed the police to attend a report of an incident in a school without being duty bound to record the crime and therefore charge the minors involved. The recording of a crime as 'Outcome 21' to a sexting crime became official advice from the College of Policing in late 2016. Police can make a record of a crime with various 'outcomes' – for example Outcome 1 is 'A person has been charged', Outcome 3 is 'An adult caution has been issued' and Outcome 19 records 'No crime'.

An Outcome 21 record states:

> *'Further investigation, resulting from the crime report, which could provide evidence sufficient to support formal action being taken against the suspect is not in the public interest – police decision.'*

This development was viewed as a progressive step forward in policing, while still being constrained by the limitations of the legislation. What was clear was there was little political will to change the law, so this was the best the police felt they could do.

However, our visits to schools around the country suggested that while this recording option was available to police officers, its application was inconsistent – some schools were aware of such recording, some were not, and many still had police talks to their pupils where the only advice was that old chestnut that is becoming so familiar, 'Don't send nudes, it's illegal'. It seemed that the application hinged on the knowledge of the school, and the attending officer, which did not fill

---

124 https://news.npcc.police.uk/releases/a-common-sense-police-approach-to-investigating-sexting-among-under-18s

us with confidence that this supposed solution would actually achieve the intended outcome.

As a result of these concerns, research was commissioned with which Andy was involved. The aim of this research was to serve a Freedom of Information request on all police forces to gauge the number of times an Outcome 21 had been recorded relating to an adolescent sexting incident, and how many times the old approach (charging under section one of the Protection of Children Act 1978) was carried out.

The data[125] suggest that there still seems to be numerous arrests of minors for these activities, and that new police powers that allow them to record a crime without it appearing formally on a young person's criminal record, were being applied disproportionately and excessively by some forces. While we will not explore the data in any detail here (the research report can be found via a link in the footnote), it was clear from the data that there was little consistency in how the new guidance, and old legislation, was being applied. In some forces there were far more Outcome 21 records than formal charges, and in some the opposite was true. However, perhaps more of a concern was the fact that in some forces, Outcome 21 recording was being conducted in far higher volumes – in one force three adolescents had been charged, and 300 had received an Outcome 21 recording.

What was clear from the research:

- Children and young people were still, in some cases, being arrested, and in some cases were minors under the age of 14.
- Outcome 21 recording is being applied by most forces, in greatly varying volumes.
- The number of Outcome 21 recordings, in more cases, far exceeds the number of arrests (in some cases there is a tenfold difference).

While one may, and should, view this as positive for young people, one should remain mindful that while it is viewed as a 'non-conviction', the

---

125 Phippen, A., and Bond, E. (2019) *Police response to youth offending around the generation and distribution of indecent images of children and its implications.* Available at: www.uos.ac.uk/sites/default/files/FOI-Report-Final-Outcome-21.pdf (Accessed 9 August 2021).

high numbers of Outcome 21 records (far more than had previously been charged) is a concern if we are to explore the wording of the police guidance, which states:

> 'The discretion on whether to disclose non-conviction information rests with each chief constable managing the process.'

In other words, should a minor with an Outcome 21 recording be in a position in later life that a DBS check[126] is needed, there is still a chance that this will still be disclosed. As can be seen with this data, major force discrepancies show Outcome 21 being applied differently across forces. Without published policy on how this discretion by chief constables is applied, a minor in one part of the country who is spoken to by the police as a result of a sexting activity might be treated differently as someone living under another police force location.

It might be assumed that Outcome 21 is being applied in far more cases because of the belief that there is no lasting impact on the young person. This is not necessarily the case, and the system risks a soft criminalisation of children who, prior to the inception of Outcome 21, were more likely to have received a telling off and told to be more mindful in the future.

How should we support young people?

The narrative around teen sexting has, for over ten years, been driven by the legality of the act and the failure to acknowledge a minor as having sexual agency or engaging in such practices as a choice. The public discourse has to centre upon the child as victim and the need to protect them from harm. There has been an almost total failure to listen to the youth voice in all of this.

A particularly troubling aspect of these discussions is that we know it is very unlikely a young person subjected to this sort of abuse would turn to an adult for help. The vast majority of young people in our research have said their peers would be the people they would ask. The idea that an adult might help, or even understand, was lost on a lot of young people

---

126 A Disclosure and Barring Service check, used to check a person's data on central police records to check on convictions in the case, for example, of them wishing to work with children.

who felt that if they were to mention such abuse to an adult, they would be 'judged' as having done something wrong (despite this practice being conducted by many adults[127]). So, in this scenario we could potentially have a vulnerable minor who is feeling isolated and alone as a result of sending an image of him or herself, which is then distributed further by the recipient, who has nowhere to turn because their expectation is they will be, at the very least, told off for doing it, and there might also be a chance they will be arrested for receiving the image in the first place. However, as we have discussed above, once past the age of majority the same individual, in the same situation, should be protected in law, rather than being threatened by it.

We can see this gross disparity as one that has always dogged prohibitive educational messages around those social activities that have some element of legal boundary. Even if we could deliver education programmes where young people engaged with the legislative position of the behaviours with which they are engaging (and given the perceived failures prohibitive approaches have had toward issues such as smoking, drinking alcohol or taking illegal narcotics[128] we might suggest that such engagement is not likely to be particularly forthcoming), we do not have a clear view with which to reassure the victims that by disclosing abuse there would be legal protection for them. Therefore, it is unsurprising that young people have little confidence with adults successfully resolving issues that arise from sexting.

We clearly have a gulf between those living a hyperconnected childhood, and those who are tasked with ensuring their safety and wellbeing, whether this be schools or parents. With a lack of understanding of the issues associated with sexting or a refusal to engage with such due to what might be perceived as professional risk on the part of the teacher (mitigating the chances of a parent being outraged as a result of a child

---

127 McAfee. (2014) *Stop! Do you really want to send that photo?* Available at: www.mcafee.com/blogs/consumer/love-and-tech (Accessed: 10 August 2021).

128 Plant, E., & Plant, M. (1999) Primary prevention for young children: a comment on the UK government's 10 year drug strategy. *International Journal of Drug Policy*, 10(5): pp. 385-401.

coming home and saying 'Sir talked to me about sexting today'), or shock on the part of the parent ('No way would my child do this') we fall back on a prohibitive ideology – 'We must stop them from doing this, then we don't have to address it in school or in the home'.

Young people need to be aware that while sexting is, in their eyes, normal, it does not mean they are expected to tolerate the resultant abuse that can arise. Victims are rarely to blame for the redistribution of an image. However, we must also be mindful that the behaviour on the part of the supposed offender is often ill conceived and lacking in malice. While it might seem unusual for someone who grew up before the advent of social media to see sending an indecent, unsolicited image as a prelude to genuine friendship, affection and romance, the dearth of pastoral education in this area means it is not an entirely unreasonable expectation for young people in the 21st century, however unwise it might appear to their parents.

Sexting is a complex issue. It is not simply a case that a child will reach a certain age then decide the best way to obtain a boyfriend or girlfriend is to take an explicit image of themselves and send it to potential partners. The practice of sexting lies in the need to be popular, to have a boyfriend/ girlfriend, to be told you look attractive, to show you are grown up and so on. It is unlikely, even when a young person has received an assembly or some classroom time where their teacher or parent has reminded them that taking and sending such an image is actually breaking the law, that in the split second when the young person decides to press the send button on their mobile device, they will refrain from doing so by being reminded that they might become criminalised as a result.

Equally, as a result of said discussion, if a young person who does press send, and is subsequently abused as a result of the image being redistributed, it is extremely unlikely they will disclose this abuse if they have been told that what they were doing was illegal and 'Once it's online it's always online'. Coupled with the lack of education around these matters, and young people's awareness that, in general, adults with caring responsibilities lack knowledge of these issues, young people turn to peers to resolve harm and mitigate risk. Obviously, this is not an ideal situation if we wish to develop a consistent, supportive knowledge base for our young people around digital safeguarding issues.

We owe young people much more than this. We are failing in the rights of children to receive effective education (Article 29 – Goals of Education in the UNCRC (UN General Assembly 1989)) given that we are failing to engage with the complexity of an area such as sexting, due to a lack of understanding of the topic at the policy and legislative level. Legislation that will protect victims, punish offenders and provide effective deterrent, while being mindful of what might arise in the future, is extremely difficult to achieve in the digital world. While it is challenging to predict which technologies will embed into society in the future, and how they will be used in the social context, it is even more problematic to apply comprehensive and complete legislation to protect those most vulnerable from harm. Equally, as we have seen with many other prohibitive ideologies, a position that uses legislation as the foundation of a preventative strategy is rarely effective.

A failure to appreciate the complex and social nature of digital harm and abuse means we risk imposing greater levels of technical surveillance and control on our young people. This would all be done in the vain hope that by doing such we will protect them. This idea of a potential safeguarding dystopia is explored in more depth in the final chapter, which also explores the growing reliance on content control, monitoring and tracking as way to ensure our children and young people are safe. In such ways are contemporary childhoods slowly and painstakingly eroded. Fortunately, this does not have to be the case, as we will explain.

Chapter 5
See everything, always

In 2018 the UK celebrity Jamie Oliver promoted[129] the use of tracking technology, saying it was a 'brilliant' way to ensure his children were safe when they were away from the family home. Mr Oliver was quoted as saying:

> 'The older girls, Jools and I are all on an app…, which means we can see exactly where everybody is and the route they've gone, so if one of the girls says, "I'm going to Camden Town" and I can see they've gone to Reading, then we have a problem.'

He continued:

> 'They can check on me, too, and see how fast I'm driving. It's brilliant.'

In this chapter we explore attitudes toward tracking and monitoring of young people's online (and offline) behaviour, and the broader view that technology causes these issues, therefore technology can solve them. While returning to tracking technologies later in this chapter, it is worthwhile to briefly reflect upon Mr Oliver's views – there seems to be a belief that knowing where their children are, the whole time, is a good thing. He knows they are apparently safe if he knows where they are. What would be Mr Oliver's response should the blinking dot on the map disappear? We are aware, through our conversations with police officers,

---

129 The Independent. (2018) *Jamie Oliver reveals he tracks daughters' location on app – but parenting experts say it could cause future problems.* Available at: www.independent.co.uk/life-style/health-and-families/jamie-oliver-tracks-location-life360-kids-parenting-a8545136. html (Accessed 9 August 2021).

that 999 calls are made because the parent can no longer see their child's blip on the map. We propose that this 'brilliant' app, in the words of Mr Oliver, does not actually provide much reassurance that the child is safe – it simply tells him where the child's device is. And is this app being used to reassure safety, or is it more a surveillance device?

This is the first generation where this sort of information is technically available to parents. Prior to the digital age, with GPS technology and easy access to location information via 'brilliant' apps, there had to be a level of trust between parent and child.

'I'm off round my friend's house.'

'OK, be back by 5 for your dinner.'

If they weren't back for dinner, there might be some issues to discuss, but the child's disclosed location was not one of them.

Being unable to know where the child was, and taking the child's information on trust, was a fundamental part of the parent/child relationship. Now, technology can provide us with more information on a child's whereabouts, interactions and communications, and even a means to record their whole day. This extreme scenario is sometimes one we offer to parents when discussing how much technical surveillance is reasonable. One could, quite easily, attach a wearable camera to a child at the start of the school day and then download the recording at the end of the day (or even set it up so it live streams) to view all of their interactions, judge the behaviour of others in the classroom, the conduct of their teachers, and so on. We would hope that readers are not now thinking 'what a brilliant idea'! While the concept is technically possible, there are, thankfully, legal safeguards in place to ensure that the recording of other children in a classroom is not *de rigueur*, as is the case for behavioural biometrics. However, we are seeing 'wearable tech' increasingly in public spaces, for example police bodycams, and we are sure it won't be long before we are asked our view on this technology in a school setting.

From our time working in schools, and particularly in parents' sessions, we can observe that there is no typical parent when it comes to technical intervention. And this chapter is neither intending to judge parental choices, nor shame a particular perspective. It is, instead, intending to provide some discussion around the origins of these technical interventions and, to some degree, explore the capabilities of the software against the claims of vendors, so that parents might make more informed judgements on both the efficacy of the technology and also some ethical reflections on what they purport to do.

Returning to our observations from parents' sessions, it is clear that some will place great faith in technological solutions and believe that with technology in place to prevent harm, there requires no further intervention. For others, a more hands-on approach to digital parenting means that they are more likely to monitor their children online, playing a more proactive role in ensuring safety from harm. Of course, there are others that fall between these two modes of parenting. Parenting styles also change over time, depending on the ages of any children.

Parents are, quite understandably, worried about their children's online lives. There is no shortage of media articles reporting on online harms, and the need for everyone to 'do more' to ensure children remain safe. A couple of years ago we were involved in some work with online forum MumsNet and the Internet Watch Foundation, which surveyed MumsNet members about their concerns.[130] We provided some input around parental controls and the sorts of technology used by parents, aiming to gain a detailed parental perspective on concerns and how they manage them.

Looking at the responses reported in the survey, the issues over 50% of parents are concerned about in relation to their children are:

- Being exposed to sexual imagery/pornography
- Bullying
- Being exposed to unpleasant or aggressive people (e.g. trolls, bad language)
- Being exposed to violent imagery
- Grooming
- Child sexual exploitation via video or photographs

130 www.mumsnet.com/child/top-online-safety-concerns-for-parents

- Deciding to meet strangers met online in real life
- Issues to do with body image and self-esteem
- Internet use interfering with sleeping patterns
- Being exposed to extremist attitudes.

With this level of parental concern, it is understandable that they might be looking for tools or help to ensure their children are *safe* online.

In addressing these concerns, parents reported a number of tools and techniques to help assure safety:

Control access to sites	47 %
Age restriction/filtering	41 %
We can see what the children look at	62 %
Children are only allowed online for a certain amount of time	48 %
Children are not allowed online after a certain time	35 %
Children are only allowed to go online in family rooms	40 %
Monitoring apps on mobile devices	17 %
Tracking apps on mobile devices	6 %

Unsurprisingly, as parental concern has grown, the has been an industry of 'solutions' that can be sold to parents to give them the reassurance they seek. The burgeoning industry in what is sometimes annoyingly referred to in the marketing phraseology of *SafetyTech*, marketed against messages that imply 'Peace of mind ensured', 'You will know that they are safe if you can see what they are doing', and 'You will know they are safe if you know where they are', offers all manner of functionalities:

- Filtering of 'inappropriate content'
- Social media monitoring (both access, screen time and even what is being typed)
- Managing screen time through either reporting or proactive management (such as shutting the device down at given times or after a set duration)
- Managing screen time on specific apps or blocking them entirely
- Accessing messaging platforms so that parents can see messages sent

- Setting a block list in contacts
- Seeing call logs
- Location tracking and 'boundary setting' – being alerted if a child strays beyond set locations
- Alerting parents around sexual communication or cyberbullying
- Accessing images the child has taken to determine whether or not they are 'appropriate'.

We should bear in mind that these tools are marketed to address issues in ensuring a child is safe when they are online – providing reassurance to parents that their child is where they claim to be, that they are not taking intimate images, or that they are not being cyberbullied. There is less in the marketing material, generally, around the rights of the child or invasions of privacy, or the balance between concern and control.

SafetyTech and the reassurance myth

Since online safeguarding has emerged onto the political landscape, and become a public interest event sufficiently high profile to attract the attention of the media, there have been calls to make use of technology to prevent the accessing of certain types of content and carrying out certain behaviours online. The simple, albeit poorly thought out, premise is due to this content or these behaviours being conducted online; 'surely' there are technical means to prevent someone from accessing certain types of content perceived to be harmful.

And as with most aspects of the online world, sadly it is rarely as simple as that. While there are aspects of digital technology that do impact upon harms – things like geographical reach, perceived (incorrectly) anonymity, scale and accessibility all play a part in the nature of online harms, most behaviours enacted that cause harms are social and human in nature – the digital world does not mean people behave in completely novel ways. They simply behave as is their nature, but online.

A famous cybersecurity researcher, Marcus Ranum, once stated:

'You can't solve social problems with software.'

This has moved into tech culture as 'Ranum's law',[131] and is frequently quoted in opposition to political and media demands to implement technology to prevent online harm from occurring. Nevertheless, the media has always had a fascination, mainly viewed negatively, around digital technology and its propensity for harm. As far back as 1999, the science fiction author Douglas Adams famously penned an essay[132] that observed the implied causation of any technology-facilitated crime in a manner that would not be levelled at other ambient factors:

'Newsreaders still feel it is worth a special and rather worrying mention if, for instance, a crime was planned by people "over the Internet." They don't bother to mention when criminals use the telephone or the M4, or discuss their dastardly plans "over a cup of tea," though each of these was new and controversial in their day.'

And we can see this view similarly in the political arena, something we will explore further in this chapter. For a long time, the technology sector has talked about the Four Horsemen of the Information Apocalypse, or Infocalypse:

'Beware the Four Horsemen of the Information Apocalypse: terrorists, drug dealers, kidnappers, and child pornographers. Seems like you can scare any public into allowing the government to do anything with those four.'[133]

While the exact nature of the Four Horsemen varies in the telling of the tale (in some versions the horsemen are organised crime, terrorists, drug dealers and paedophiles), the observation remains the same – in order to win over public opinion about the regulation of specific aspects of technology, it is necessary to show them how one or more of the Horsemen make use of the technology. This will be picked up by the

---

131 Cheswick, W. R. et al. (2003) *Firewalls and internet security: repelling the wily hacker.* Boston: Addison-Wesley Professional. p. 202.

132 Adams, D. (1999) *How to stop worrying and learn to love the internet.* Available at: https://douglasadams.com/dna/19990901-00-a.html (Accessed: 9 August 2021).

133 Schneier, B. (2005) 'Computer crime hype', *Schneier on security,* 16 December 2005 [Blog]. Available at: www.schneier.com/blog/archives/2005/12/computer_crime_1.html (Accessed: 9 August 2021).

media to propagate the message of harm by one of these Horsemen, and public opinion (essential to win over support for regulation and control) will fall in behind the intended political direction. We have seen this many times over the years, most recently with growing opposition to Facebook's proposal to use end-to-end encryption, a technique to ensure a message cannot be intercepted and read by a third party, on their messenger platforms.[134]

The response from a number of Western law enforcement agencies and governments is that this would be a bad idea.[135] A co-signed open letter by Priti Patel, UK Home Secretary, William P. Barr, United States Attorney General, Kevin K. McAleenan, United States Acting Secretary of Homeland Security and Peter Dutton MP, Australian Minister for Home Affairs[136] to Mark Zuckerberg, Facebook's CEO on 4 October 2019 showed that current political rhetoric still focuses on the need for 'exceptional access' to encrypted communication – they were asking the technology providers to place 'backdoors' into encrypted communications such that, in the event of criminal concern, law enforcement might be able to break the encryption and read the messages.

The typical approach to digital encryption has remained fairly consistent for a long time – it uses mathematical techniques to encode a message or other form of information so it can only be accessed by authorised parties and is unreadable to those who are not (for example, those who may intercept it). While it cannot prevent interference, it does prevent the interceptor being able to decipher the message and get any meaning from it. In a typical encryption scenario, a message, the *plaintext*, is encrypted using an algorithm to generate *ciphertext* that can then only be read if it is decrypted. In most encryption algorithms a key is used to encrypt the

---

134 https://about.fb.com/news/2019/03/vision-for-social-networking/

135 www.wired.com/story/encryption-wars-facebook-messaging/

136 Patel, P. et al. (2019) *Open letter from the Home Secretary – alongside US Attorney General Barr, Secretary of Homeland Security (Acting) McAleenan, and Australian Minister for Home Affairs Dutton – to Mark Zuckerberg.* Available at: www.gov.uk/government/publications/ open-letter-to-mark-zuckerberg/open-letter-from-the-home-secretary-alongside-us-attorney-general-barr-secretary-of-homeland-security-acting-mcaleenan-and-australian-minister-f (Accessed: 10 August 2021).

message, which is generally a randomly (or pseudo-randomly) generated piece of data that can be mathematically applied to the plaintext to produce the ciphertext. Different schemes operate in different ways in order to decrypt, but generally the recipient requires either the same key, or part of a key pair, in order to convert the message back into plaintext. While it is mathematically possible to break the ciphertext without the key, it requires considerable computing resources because it essentially requires a guessing of the decryption key. The larger the key, the more difficult it is to discover at random.

A backdoor in an encryption process is a method to bypass the usual method of authentication (i.e. being in possession of the key to decrypt). A backdoor would allow a third party to access the encrypted information either by means of guessing the key or having a 'skeleton key' that would also allow decryption. Fundamentally, a backdoor causes encryption's essence to fail – it is no longer a private communication between two parties. It becomes a communication a third party can access. As control of the nature of the third party is not something one can implement in software code, software has little capability to subjectively interpret the intentions of the third party – are they a law enforcement operative, a government official, or a criminal? Introducing a backdoor means knowledge of it allows the encryption to be broken by any third party.

Government attempts to allow access to encrypted communications are nothing new; there have been attempts to control encryption harking back to the 1970s, often referred to as the 'Crypto Wars'.[137] Nevertheless, the high-profile report of Facebook's intention to encrypt all communications seems to have done exactly that. Returning to the open letter to Facebook, the authors made it clear that if Facebook were to move to end-to-end encryption, they would be helping various criminal activities [bold has been added by us for emphasis]:

> *'You stated that "we have a responsibility to work with law enforcement and to help prevent" the use of Facebook for things like* **child sexual exploitation, terrorism, and extortion.**

---

137 www.eff.org/document/crypto-wars-governments-working-undermine-encryption

...

Companies should not deliberately design their systems to preclude any form of access to content, even for preventing or investigating the most serious crimes. This puts our citizens and societies at risk by severely eroding a company's ability to detect and respond to illegal content and activity, such as child sexual exploitation and abuse, terrorism, and foreign adversaries' attempts to undermine democratic values and institutions, preventing the prosecution of offenders and safeguarding of victims.'

While a political message such as 'We want to undermine encryption because we want to snoop on your communications' might not be palatable, saying instead 'Paedophiles use this technology to hide their activities and we cannot do anything about it, so do you think it's a good idea to ban it?' is far more likely to win over public opinion. It's all in the phrasing of the question.

However, the failing of this argument is that it considers end-to-end encryption as a new technology being applied for the first time. However, as we have highlighted, this has been a debate that has raged since the 1970s and end-to-end encryption is implemented in many messaging platforms already.

At the time of writing, the following messaging apps, all freely available, implement end-to-end encryption:

- Apple iMessage
- WhatsApp
- ViberLine
- Telegram
- KakaoTalk
- Signal
- Dust
- Wickr
- Cyphr
- CoverMe

- Silence
- Pryvate Now
- SureSpot
- Wire

In summary, sometimes, with the best of intentions, governments get this stuff wrong. However, they are far less likely to back down from a policy direction once undertaken, and this is true when we consider SafetyTech. There has been, and remains, a view that technology will be able to solve all manner of social issues that arise online. While it began with demands such as 'Stop children viewing pornography', we can see many examples of the view that technology could tackle all manner of online social issues, centring around technology companies providing *solutions* to ensure children are safe from the variety of risks associated with going online. For example, in recent years we have had a number of calls, such as:

- The UK Health Secretary calling for algorithms to be installed onto children's mobile phones to detect indecent images and prevent them from being sent[138]
- Legislation to impose age verification technology on anyone wishing to access pornography from a UK based device[139]
- Calls to extend age verification onto social media sites to ensure no-one under 13 can access these services and for social media companies to ensure children cannot access their services for more than two hours per day[140]

---

138 House of Commons. (2019) *Impact of social media and screen-use on young people's health*. Available at: www.publications.parliament.uk/pa/cm201719/cmselect/cmsctech/822/822.pdf (Accessed: 10 August 2021).

139 Legislation.gov.uk. (2017) *Digital economy act 2017*. Available at: www.legislation.gov.uk/ukpga/2017/30/part/3/enacted (Accessed: 10 August 2021).

140 The Observer. (2018) *Health chiefs to set social media time limits for young people*. Available at: www.theguardian.com/media/2018/sep/29/health-chief-set-social-media-time-limits-young-people (Accessed: 10 August 2021).

- Calls for social media companies to stop the live streaming of terrorist activities[141]
- Calls for social media companies to prevent the posting of 'anti-vax' materials.[142]

Yet calling for something does not actually mean it is possible. Technology can only ever be a tool of support to broader social context from these issues. There are some things that digital technology is very good at in this area:

- Reporting routes and responsive, and transparent, take downs
- Warnings around content based upon keyword analysis and, in some cases, image comparison
- Pre-screening of some content that is easily identifiable as it has been previously classified
- Monitoring network access and raising alerts using rule-based systems, for example, on a known website that provides access to harmful content
- The means to block abusers
- Interpreting new data based upon its similarity to previous data it has been shown.

However, there are other things that technology is far less good at:

- Inference of context of textual content
- Identification of content outside of clearly defined heuristics
- Image processing in a broad and subjective context (for example 'indecency')
- Subjective interpretation of meaning and nuance in textual data.

---

141 BBC. (2019) *Christchurch shootings: Sajid Javid warns tech giants over footage*. Available at: www.bbc.co.uk/news/uk-47593536 (Accessed: 10 August 2021).

142 The Guardian. (2019) *Matt Hancock 'won't rule out' compulsory vaccinations*. Available at: www.theguardian.com/politics/2019/may/04/matt-hancock-wont-rule-out-compulsory-vaccinations (Accessed: 10 August 2021).

Digital technology is very good at clearly defined, rule-based functionality in easily contained system boundaries. Or, to put it another way, data processing, analysis, and pattern matching of data. Computers are very good at taking data and analysing it based upon rules defined within the system (for example, identify words that *might* relate to sexual content). What they are far less good at is interpretation, *intelligence*, and inference. With SafetyTech, sometimes the expectations outweigh the capability.

If we are to consider the sorts of technical approaches available to those who want to implement some form of SafetyTech they generally fall into three categories:

1. Filtering – preventing access to certain types of content online (pornography, gambling, terrorist materials, etc).

2. Monitoring – looking at the types of interactions being carried out on a device/network, for example looking at access data, measuring and limiting time spent online, intercepting and reading communications, live intervention on communications, etc.

3. Tracking – using location-based technologies to locate and follow an individual/device.

In the remainder of this chapter, we will consider the origins of each of these classes of intervention and their ideological origins.

SafetyTech – filtering

Filtering technologies have been well established in schools for many years. The basic approach is a simple one – prevent access to 'inappropriate' web content that might be harmful, upsetting or offensive for young people. In schools most of the systems use keyword matching and blocking at a web address level to detect 'inappropriate' content (schools have a statutory duty to implement 'appropriate' filtering and monitoring of their online systems). So, put simply, the system looks for sexual keywords and blocks access to sites that contain them, or it checks against a list of sites already blocked, to prevent access should someone attempt to access that website. While the system is not perfect (many young people have told us they have experienced the filtering systems blocking innocent websites), it is accepted as a useful tool in school settings. However, filtering has now moved into the home domain, with current political fascination in the UK (as illustrated by the current Online Harms White Paper[143] and recently published draft Online Safety Bill[144]) viewing filters as a solution to prevent access to 'harmful' content in the home.

One of the fundamental issues with home filtering is how restrictive it can become, particularly when it makes use of keyword matching. As stated above, algorithms are poor at recognising context, therefore it will identify the word and block, regardless of the ambiguity of the use of the word. By way of an illustrative, albeit trivial, example, let us take the word 'cock'. This is a term that might be related to a sexual context – it could refer colloquially to male genitalia. Equally, it might refer to a male chicken. If we consider this from the perspective of a filtering system, which might be tasked with ensuring an end user cannot access websites of a sexual nature, we might provide that system with a list of keywords that could indicate sexual content. It would be expected that 'cock' may be one of these terms. The filtering system will be very good at matching this word on websites and would successfully block access to this content. However, if the site was about, for example, animal husbandry, the block would not prevent a child from accessing sexual content.

Even with this simple example, we can see how it might struggle to prevent access to all sexual content or, equally, result in *false positives* – blocking innocuous[145] sites that are not 'inappropriate' for children to see (often referred to as overblocking). Another simple and popular example of overblocking comes from frequent restriction on access to web content related to the Northern English town of Scunthorpe,[146] given that a substring of its composition is a vulgar word for female genitalia.

---

143 www.gov.uk/government/consultations/online-harms-white-paper
144 www.gov.uk/government/publications/draft-online-safety-bill
145 We will use the term 'innocuous' to describe those sites that have been incorrectly blocked based upon the requirements of the filter (for example, pornography, gambling, drugs and alcohol) and not 'legal', because access to pornography is legal in the UK.
146 Wikipedia. (2021) Scunthorpe problem. Available at: https://en.wikipedia.org/wiki/Scunthorpe_problem (Accessed: 10 August 2021).

At the time of writing in the UK, the opposition party[147] has just made a call for social media platforms to prevent the spreading of 'anti-vax' misinformation and the need to 'stamp out' such information. They argued that emergency laws would hold platforms responsible should they fail to take down false stories about emerging Covid-19 vaccination programmes. Platforms, they stated, should be held financially and criminally liable if they fail in their *duty of care* to remove such information.

However, as with any rule-based approach to content blocking, there needs to be a clear legal definition. Without a legal definition it would be virtually impossible for an algorithm to accurately block this sort of information. Would content questioning government policy be considered 'anti-vax'? Or a comment criticising vaccine policy in a given country? It is very easy for someone (usually a politician) to say 'This should be stopped' without actually thinking through what, technically, that would mean.

The differentiation of the legal and illegal is a complex one and we can see differences in success between attempts to block each. Illegal content is well managed through services such as that run by the Internet Watch Foundation. This organisation has been granted proactive powers by the government to search for websites that provide access to child abuse material. When it is detected it is either (if in the UK) taken down and legal proceedings against the provider are launched, or the website address is added to the IWF watchlist of sites providing access to illegal material. Providing internet access that scans the IWF URL list means that illegal content related to child abuse can be effectively managed and it is unlikely that even the most freedom craving internet libertarian would argue that this material should be accessed in a café WiFi hotspot or in the home. However, other forms of content blocking become more problematic, and face similar problems of overblocking that a lot of other filtering services face, which we will address in more detail below.

147 BBC. (2020) *Covid-19: Stop anti-vaccination fake news online with new law says Labour*. Available at: www.bbc.co.uk/news/uk-politics-54947661 (Accessed: 10 August 2021).

Returning to the more general issue around the introduction of filters in the home, there is general agreement that the year that filtering in the home became easily available was 2013, when the government pressured the four main internet service providers into putting 'default on' filtering tools into their home packages. Therefore, home filtering has now been widely available to subscribers for almost ten years. In the parents' survey above with MumsNet subscribers, as well as data from young people we surveyed,[148] we can see that around 40% of parents chose to have filters switched on. Ofcom's Media Literacy report 2018[149] reports a figure of 34% of parents of 5 to 15-year-olds installing filters. While we do not have much data on why parents do not choose to install them at home, the low numbers, after almost ten years of being available, do raise the question – if these technologies are effective, why wouldn't parents install them in the home?

SafetyTech – monitoring

In extending the discussion to the other primary safeguarding tool to control access to inappropriate content, we will now consider the nature of monitoring – generally viewed as the more progressive, and less restrictive, bedfellow to filtering. A basic monitoring approach is to use software to look at network traffic and raise alerts when monitoring rules are breached. While monitoring approaches will adopt similar techniques to filtering initially (for example, triggering an alert if someone generated a monitored keywork or tries to access a website on a watchlist) monitoring's toolbox can extend far beyond this. For example, message interaction and sharing, the interception, identification and redistribution of images, and elucidation of intent in communications based upon algorithmic interpretation. The title of this chapter draws upon the advertising strapline for a monitoring SafetyTech provider.

---

148 Phippen, A. (2019) *Young people, internet use and wellbeing: Technology in the home.* Available at: www.swgfl.org.uk/assets/documents/technology-in-the-home.pdf (Accessed: 10 August 2021).

149 Ofcom. (2019) *Children and parents' media use and attitudes: Annex 1.* Available at: www.ofcom.org.uk/__data/assets/pdf_file/0027/134892/Children-and-Parents-Media-Use-and-Attitudes-Annex-1.pdf (Accessed: 10 August 2021).

They propose that their technology allows the parent to *See Everything, Always*. This is the proposed power of monitoring systems.

Monitoring has evolved from a school-centric technology to one that is also pervasive in the home and into the digital home, and family life. The central concept of any monitoring approach is simple – collect data on online access at a network or application level, and develop response strategies accordingly. As with filtering, schools have an expectation under the Keeping Children Safe in Education statutory guidance[150] to have *appropriate* monitoring in place. And as with filtering, the guidance on what *appropriate* is, is defined outside of the statutory duties.

Within the school setting, the basic URL/keyword monitoring has now been superseded with other more active/proactive platforms that can work at a far more sophisticated level. An example might be engaging in proactive monitoring while a pupil is typing, and making judgements on their intention as a result of this. There is clear guidance that, within a school setting, the technology will not be an automated solution, but a tool to support staff in making safeguarding judgements. Which is, arguably, the best role for technology – to collect data, raise alerts, and leave decision making to other stakeholders.

However, there has been significant evidence of feature creep[151] in monitoring systems, particularly with home and app-based systems. While they used to function mainly around list-based interception and alerts, the technical capabilities of software and network systems means that the feature suite can now be far more complex. But, with the introduction of new features there seems to be little checking on whether, just because technology makes something possible, it *should* become part of a monitoring system. And there seems to be even less evidence of consideration of children's rights around these features and raises the question – when does a monitor become surveillance?

---

150 Department for education. (2021) *Statutory guidance: Keeping children safe in education*. Available at: www.gov.uk/government/publications/ keeping-children-safe-in-education--2 (Accessed: 10 August 2021).
151 https://en.wikipedia.org/wiki/Feature_creep

A good example of excessive monitoring can be seen in a famous legal case in the US – *Robbins v. Lower Merion School District*.[152] This case has been subject to much discussion and is worthwhile exploring here because it does highlight the issue of technology extending moral boundaries and excessive control. In this case a number of schools in the Lower Merion School District in the US adopted a policy of providing pupils with laptops for both in-school and at-home use. The expectation that the school might adopt a safeguarding approach that would use some forms of technology to monitor laptop usage is reasonable, and they need to mitigate risk around the devices potentially being used for social or even illegal activities.

However, the software the schools decided to install far exceeded this intent. As a result of one of the schools involved in the scheme disciplining a pupil for what they referred to as 'inappropriate' behaviour at home, it was discovered that the laptops were not only monitoring internet access and application usage, but were also sending a stream of images back to the school servers for analysis by staff.

As a result of suspicions raised by Blake Robbins, the pupil being disciplined, it was finally determined that over 66,000 images of pupils at his school were collected via these devices using the built-in webcams on the laptops. As well as sending images to the school directly when an online connection was available, the monitoring software was also capable of collecting images locally and uploading them at a later time. While the school argued they had valid safeguarding reasons for collecting this data, it was clear from the case that consent had not been obtained. Even if there was a safeguarding concern, the fact that the image data was subsequently used in a pupil disciplinary, clearly demonstrated this remit had far been exceeded without fair consideration of the pupil's privacy or data protection rights.

Furthermore, it was argued that given the schools took a *proactive* decision not to inform either pupils or parents of the installed monitoring software or request consent, there is evidence that the intention was covert and pupil's privacy had further been breached.

---

152 www.pacermonitor.com/view/6LZS7RA/ROBBINS_et_al_v_LOWER_
MERION_SCHOOL_DISTRICT_et__paedce-10-00665__0001.0.pdf

Unsurprisingly, the case found against the school district, and they were subject to a significant fine. This case was one of the first to highlight the potential for abuse in a monitoring system, and the temptation for excessive data collection just because the technology made this possible. It would be doubtful that, for example, the software platform used would have been advertised as 'Collect images of children in their home and use this data to discipline them in school'.

While there are concerns about excessive monitoring and abuse of technology in schools there is at least reassurance that statutory instruments and legislation such as Data Protection mean that there should be safeguards in place to ensure that inappropriate use and abuse of data might be controlled and even punished. However, this is not the case in the home setting.

One aspect of SafetyTech that has more recently been added to the monitoring toolkit, and one that has become mainstream very quickly, is the measurement of screen time. Most smartphones will now provide screen time measures for the device users, and there are many tools that provide the means for parents to both view, and control, screen time for children. As a tool for controlling access, the tools tend to work well, although we would raise the need to discuss with young people agreed screen time limits, rather than punitive imposition, and there are many reasons why limiting screen time might be a positive tool. However, a common thread through this text is the many failures of this area to engage effectively with evidence, and the role of misinformation in raising alarm when perhaps none exists. One of these areas is the myth that excessive screen time = increased harm or negative impact upon mental health. Frankly, there is insufficient evidence to state either case.

It is frequently suggested, such as in the Online Harms White Paper, that parents need tools to ensure their children are not online excessively. However, there seems to be little understanding of what *excessive* means – it seems to be an entirely arbitrary and subjective term. In the past there seemed to have been similar concerns as to how long young people watched television. Again, there seemed to be little rigorous evidence to support any claims made, but there was much discourse around how watching television was a passive, negative activity, and young people would be better off playing outside. When we (as we frequently have been) are asked by parents 'How long should my child be online for per day?' our rather annoying response is usually 'How long do you think they should be online for?' Another, equally irritating, response is 'It depends'. Screen time could be passive consumption of content on platforms such as YouTube and TikTok. Alternatively, they could be spending their time online collaboratively building a new extension to a *Roblox* game, developing technology knowledge and skills, and interacting actively with peers. Therefore, simplistic proposals to 'manage' screen time are sometimes unhelpful. But, nevertheless, these proposals are made.

In an interview in the *Times* on Saturday 10 March 2018,[153] the then Secretary of State for Digital, Culture, Media and Sport, Matt Hancock, announced plans to bring in legislation that would restrict the amount of time children and young people could use social media platforms online in a simple soundbite:

> *'There is a genuine concern about the amount of screen time young people are clocking up and the negative impact it might have on their lives. It is right that we think about what more we could do in this area.'*

The broader context of the suggestion proposed a legal requirement for social media providers to put effective age verification in place for anyone over the age of 13 (with the ill-informed belief that no children are on social media platforms before this age because it's 'illegal') and to keep track of their usage, enabling legally defined limits of access to be put in place.

Mr Hancock went on to state that, in an unsurprising sense of *déjà vu*:

> *'We are not afraid to legislate because it is our job to make sure laws are up to date.'*

Yet the evidence base around the relationship between young people's use of digital technology, the time they spend online, and its impact

---

153 The Times. (2018) *Time limits for children hooked on social media.*
Available at: www.thetimes.co.uk/article/time-limits-for-children-hooked-on-social-media-3s66vwgct (Accessed: 10 August 2021).

upon their wellbeing, is very immature and poorly understood. For many years the American Association of Paediatrics (AAP) established '2+2' guidance, which was viewed as the viable measure for screen time.[154] This simply stated, with little empirical evidence, that children under two should not be online at all, and those between the ages of two and 16 should have a maximum of two hours. In a lot of the issues associated with online child safeguarding and protection, there are many who want simple answers regardless of how complex things are in reality. While in recent times the AAP have revised this view to something more complex,[155] the 2+2 is still often quoted as fact, rather than a recommendation based upon a shallow evidence base.

Our own work with children and young people would suggest quite clearly that there is a *correlation* between the amount of time a child spends online and their exposure to risk.[156] We have seen from a large dataset that children who spend a self-reported more than six hours a day online are twice as likely to have seen content or received comments that have upset them compared to someone who spends less than an hour online. It also shows that many young people who go online for over six hours a day are likely to do so because they are lonely. However, this is a correlation, not a causation and does not show whether children are lonely because they are online, or whether they are lonely, and therefore go online. Equally, we can also see from our data that there are other heavy online users who are very happy (generally these would be self-disclosed gamers).

Considering the evidence base around screen time and youth mental health, there was a large 2017 study by Andrew Przybylski and Netta

---

154 Graber, D. (2016) *Screen time and kids: Pediatricians work on a new prescription.* Available at: www.huffingtonpost.com/diana-graber/screen-time-and-kids-pedi_b_8224342.html (Accessed: 10 August 2021).

155 www.aacap.org/AACAP/Families_and_Youth/Facts_for_Families/FFF-Guide/Children-And-Watching-TV-054.aspx

156 Phippen, A. (2018) *Young people, internet use and wellbeing.* Available at: www.swgfl.org.uk/assets/documents/young-people-internet-use-and-wellbeing.pdf (Accessed: 10 August 2021).

Weinstein[157] of 120,000+ UK teens. The authors found that for 15-year-olds the effect of screen time on mental wellbeing depended on the category of screen time, and was different for weekdays and weekends. It also noted that clear negative associations with screen time were far smaller than, for example, positive associations between wellbeing and eating breakfast regularly. While young people might report on wellbeing issues we might relate to screen time, without exposure to a (probably unobtainable) full set of measures that might have an impact upon wellbeing we cannot confidently say that screen time is the causal negative factor. A more recent large-scale study by Amy Orben and Andrew Przybylski[158] argued that their data (which was multinational and detailed) showed little evidence of a link between screen time and wellbeing.

Reflecting again on our own experiences talking to children and young people, we also see many positives for screen time. For some children, for example those in isolated communities, going online is a window to the wider world. At the time of writing, we are emerging in the UK from the third national lockdown as a result of Covid-19, and many young people have disclosed the lifeline that digital technology offered them.

For those wishing to explore sexuality and gender, in small communities finding peers is a challenge, whereas going online they can find many providing them with supportive, positive and useful information. Coming out in a small town can still be challenging and has the potential to lead to serious physical harm for a young person. Being out online means they can talk with like-minded people without risk of being harmed by the less tolerant within their own communities.

For disabled children, being online might sometimes be a lifeline to an outside world. We recall a young man with severe autistic traits telling us

---

157 Przybylski, A. K., and Weinstein, N. (2017) 'A large-scale test of the Goldilocks hypothesis: Quantifying the relations between digital-screen use and the mental well-being of adolescents.' *Psychological science*, 28(2): pp. 204-215.

158 Orben, A., and Przybylski, A. K. (2019) 'Screens, teens, and psychological well-being: Evidence from three time-use-diary studies.' *Psychological science*, 30(5): pp. 682-696.

in the real world he was a coward but online he could be a hero – he loved to play *Minecraft* online with a large community of online friends for this reason. Those who struggle with direct contact with others, or who are near or completely non-verbal, find an outlet for communication with online interaction. Those with physical disabilities might not be able to go out and socialise but they can do so online and it can have a highly positive impact upon their wellbeing. Is Mr Hancock really saying that the UK Government knows better about how much time these children should spend online and how it would most positively impact upon their wellbeing than the children themselves or their parents?

We are not stating that young people should be free to be online for as long as they wish, with no control over this. However, what we would take exception to is that technology has to provide the solution to this. Surely, a more realistic approach to excessive screen time (however this is agreed in the home) is for a parent to manage it, through observation and house rules, rather than expecting technology to shut down a device for them after the application of a rule set that has little grasp of types of screen time, just minutes online.

There are a number of issues arising from this list of solutions that cause concern beyond the current screen time debate. We have already discussed filtering at length, but the proposed functionality in the feature list of home monitoring solutions far outweighs proportionate response to child safeguarding concerns. It would seem that many parents, in order to reassure themselves that their children are safe, feel they need to know about every element of communication in their lives. And SafetyTech providers can potentially build an effective business model on the back of a *reassurance myth* that will encourage parents to purchase their products, whether or not there is a real problem to solve.

We know, from many conversations with parents, that there are plenty who believe it is their right to see every conversation their child has online and to know exactly who they are speaking to at any time – the belief being if they can see all of the communications, they will know they are safe. In order to ensure they are safe online, it is *essential* that parents can access all communications. This is the first generation where this has been possible via technology. However, just because we can, is it acceptable that we do? There is a risk that we are confusing safety with surveillance, and because technology provides the methods to achieve this, we collect a suite of tools that allow us to collect more and more data on our children – convinced with the notion that they are, in some way, safe if we have all of this data.

However, as we point out frequently when delivering parent talks, what about those interactions that do not take place via a piece of technology? What about the offline interactions? If the parent is concerned about their child being bullied, it is far more likely that this will occur in the school playground, and also far more likely that the child might come to physical harm as a result. There may be a view that in a playground situation there is a devolved monitoring responsibility on the part of school staff. However, one might also observe that one teacher in a playground with many children does not guarantee interception of harm.

The concept of safety is interesting in this context – the justification for the use of increased monitoring is that it is needed to *assure* safety. In the same way that overblocking is justified because it will *prevent* access to inappropriate content. Yet do these technologies do much to actually achieve safety? Will using these tools ensure a child is safe? Or are they tools to monitor and control behaviour instead, much like we say in the Lower Merion District case? There are some risks that can be mitigated using this level of surveillance – for example the issues around grooming and contact from potential abusers might be mitigated by having access to contact lists and messaging. Yet these apps will only provide access to certain messaging platforms. While access to the mobile device's own telephony (i.e. calls and SMS) is relatively straightforward, to access app-specific messaging is more problematic, which is generally why only major platforms (for example Facebook, Instagram, Snapchat, WhatsApp) are covered.

We would ask whether the impact on children's rights is worthwhile? This impact does have some bearing on whether monitoring and tracking is performed in a covert way. We have met parents who install monitoring systems upon the children's devices after having a family discussion about why they are doing this. However, we have also spoken with parents who will adopt a more clandestine perspective on the monitoring of their children's online lives, sometimes excused with the rationale that if the children know they are being monitored, they will modify their behaviour or find ways to bypass the tools!

Monitoring does raise some interesting tensions between safeguarding and children's rights. Regardless of the approach, there are some very real impacts on privacy, in particular as a result of these tools, but also on rights such as freedom of expression and access to the media and, in the case of covert monitoring, placing significant restriction on respecting the views of the child.

By way of illustration, a BBC News report in 2019[159] had a parent justifying their own approach to the question they had posed of 'So how can we keep them safe from harmful content?' It seems, in the case of this article (and this resonates with our own conversations with some parents), it is to look at everything they do online:

'My two daughters, aged 11 and 13, loudly protest about "violations of privacy" when they realised I could see every site and app they've visited.

Once I've reassured them that this is not about snooping, but more about limitation and safety, they grudgingly seem to accept the new controls.'

SafetyTech – tracking

Moving on from monitoring of communication, the biggest change in monitoring technology in recent times has been the use of Global Positioning System (GPS) tracking technology implemented in either dedicated physical devices (such as trackable wristbands) or as a function of a mobile device. We speak to increasing numbers of children and young people who have some level of tracking by their parents. While techniques might differ, the premise is the same – the parent will install an app, or enable a tracking function on a device, which allows them to see where the child is, generally via mapping software, as was discussed at the start of this chapter in the reporting of celebrity Jamie Oliver's use of tracking technology. In general, those children who are being tracked

---

159 BBC. (2019) *How can you stop your kids viewing harmful web content?* Available at: www.bbc.co.uk/news/business-47853554 (Accessed: 11 August 2021).

that we have spoken to are fairly accepting of it – they feel it keeps the parents reassured that they are safe, and they do not feel it restricts their own behaviour. However, this does change considerably as young people get older.

Those peers who are not being tracked will generally be more concerned and, in general, pleased that they are not subjected to such surveillance (or questioned whether they are). It is also of interest to note that among the pupils at universities, we see that there are many pupils who are accepting of tracking by partners, rather than parents. With such emergent technology, it is difficult to make any inferences around whether those comfortable being tracked by partners were also tracked by parents. However, there is a general view that because the technology exists, why not use it? We would also question whether there is any reassurance of safety among those tracking partners. While some will try to justify that it is because they trust each other and want to provide reassurance, there are others who suggest the opposite is true, and it demonstrates a removal of trust in a relationship, replaced instead with surveillance. We must, once again, reflect upon whether the safeguarding justification for the use of such technology is borne out in the application, or whether this is once again part of the reassurance myths.

We were recently party to a story, shared by a safeguarding professional, of a parent upset with their 17-year-old daughter who had claimed to be visiting a (female) friend when she was actually at her boyfriend's house. The parents were annoyed their daughter had lied to them, but disclosed that they felt powerless to deliver any form of punishment. When asked why they could not punish their daughter they said that their daughter was not aware she was being tracked and if they were to tell her off then she would realise this is happening. Within this simple scenario we have a dichotomy between safety and control. Clearly the daughter was safe – she was with her boyfriend. This meant that the parents would have struggled to justify this covert tracking as a means to reassure themselves she was safe. The annoyance that she had chosen not to tell them where she was going seemed to be the fundamental concern in this scenario, which would move the justification of covert tracking from concerns about safety to retention of control. And the wish that they had decided, in the balance, that further covert tracking was preferable to making her aware of her being tracked, further demonstrates some problematic attitudes in the familial relationship.

In another discussion with an Early Years practitioner, we were told that at the end of a typical morning session at the practitioner's setting, a parent commented that she was disappointed to observe that the children had not been taken outside until mid-morning on such a lovely sunny day. When the practitioner asked the parent how she knew this, she said her child wore a trackable device which she monitored at home.

Again, a safeguarding justification for the use of this technology seems tenuous. The child is in a secure setting with trained professionals within an *in loco parentis* responsibility. Given the physical security of the setting, alongside the policies in place to manage the arrival and collection of children, it was arguably a more secure environment than a child at home playing in the garden. Yet the parent still felt the need to reassure themselves that the child was safe and, as it turned out, use the technology to make judgements on practice within the setting. It would be difficult to justify the tracking technology from a safety perspective (aside from unrealistic concerns about abduction from the setting), and the technology was clearly being used to monitor not only the child but the setting too. As a result of this incident the setting now has a policy that trackable devices are left at the door when the child arrives in the morning.

It is interesting to note that guidance from the UK Sentencing Council[160] has begun to explicitly refer to GPS tracking as evidence of coercion and control in relationships and in a domestic abuse case it might be used as a justification for a longer sentence. Yet there are some who see it as perfectly reasonable to track their children as a reassurance that they are safe (and arguably so they have control over their movements and can use the data collected as a means for discipline).

---

160 Sentencing Council. (2018) *Overarching principles: Domestic abuse.* Available at: www.sentencingcouncil.org.uk/wp-content/uploads/ Overarching-Principles-Domestic-Abuse-definitive-guideline-Web.pdf (Accessed: 11 August 2021).

To reflect upon the justification due to fear of abduction, would this technology prevent this from happening? The technology does not show where the child is, it shows where the *device* is. Someone wishing to abduct a child with knowledge of trackable devices could dispose of them in the event of an abduction. Moreover, if a parent is monitoring their child remotely, watching a dot move around a map, the physical distance means that the safeguarding reassurance may not be as effective in the event of an unexpected turn of events. If, for example, the child was 40 miles away, and then the blinking dot on the map began to accelerate further from the home location, how might the parent address this safety concern? Perhaps the first response might be to call the child, but what would then happen if the child did not answer? Would the next phase of this scenario be contacting law enforcement to say that their child is too far away or, in the event of the dot disappearing completely, missing?

There are some scenarios where it would seem proportionate to use tracking technology in a positive manner, perhaps even empowering the young person. For example, where a child suffers from a medical condition such as epilepsy where they might suffer from blackouts. In this case the tracking technology might actually be empowering – they gain a certain level of freedom by being able to be away from the family home, and all parties are comfortable in the knowledge that in the event of seizure, the young person could be located.

However, this technology is also applied far too easily in the familial relationship as a safeguarding measure with an undertone that sounds sinister if presented in a peer-to-peer relationship: 'I love you and want to know you're safe, so I need to track you.' Again, this is another technology where the reassurance myth can be used to exert more control over the child – as can be seen in the example above, it was not concern because the parents felt their daughter was unsafe, but anger because she had disobeyed them.

The reality of the reassurance myth

The cybersecurity expert Bruce Schneier, in 2006, observed the impact of surveillance on the population as a whole:

'For if we are observed in all matters, we are constantly under threat of correction, judgment, criticism, even plagiarism of our own uniqueness. We become children, fettered under watchful eyes, constantly fearful that – either now or in the uncertain future – patterns we leave behind will be brought back to implicate us, by whatever authority has now become focused upon our once-private and innocent acts. We lose our individuality, because everything we do is observable and recordable.'[161]

If one is already a child, and subject to such high and visible levels of surveillance, one can only assume an even greater docility as a result. There is, however, a fundamental flaw in this reliance on technology to survey and monitor young people, albeit for the best of intentions (sometimes). Those who wish to control need to bear in mind that the digital surveillance is easier to break out of than physical monitoring. Our conversations with young people would highlight that if they know they are being monitored, they will attempt to circumvent this. From our own work we have seen evidence that almost 50% of Year 4 children (age 7-8) disclose they know ways to work around at least some home controls.[162]

They will find ways to do this, whether this will be using a different device, making use of proxying or encryption, or even something as simple as switching the device off (in the case of being aware they are being tracked). While the information, and power imbalance, are afforded to the parent by the tools at their disposal, the knowledge gap that exists between child and parent can also be balanced in favour of the young people, and therefore they find ways to bypass the technology.

In considering the role of technology in the safeguarding toolkit, there is certainly much that can be applied in a positive manner. Filtering is certainly effective at preventing younger children from accidentally

---

161 Schneier, B. (2006) *The eternal value of privacy*. Available at: www. schneier.com/essays/archives/2006/05/the_eternal_value_of.html (Accessed: 25 August 2021).

162 Phippen, A. (2019) *Young people, internet use and wellbeing: Technology in the home*. Available at: www.swgfl.org.uk/assets/documents/technology-in-the-home.pdf (Accessed: 11 August 2021).

stumbling across upsetting content. However, it is far less likely to prevent the determined teenager from accessing pornography. And monitoring has a place in being less preventative than filtering at understanding what is being accessed and whether there should be concerns. We can even see there are some benefits for tracking technology and there are potential scenarios where the tools might be used to empower a young person.

However, as is most of what we discuss in this book, it's complicated. The SafetyTech industry will undoubtedly wish to convince parents that their tools are the solution to ensuring their children are safe, not being bullied, and always where they should be. However, they are less likely to talk about issues of trust, the need for discussion and an awareness of children's rights. Do we really need to see everything, always? Or do we instead need our children to feel empowered such that, if they do encounter something upsetting online, or are being asked to do something that makes them uncomfortable, they have the confidence to disclose it, and be confident that adults in their lives will be able to help? While the current political winds suggest the technology can provide the answers to these issues, we can say with some confidence and experience this is not the case. As we have discussed in this chapter, technology is very good at many things. Understanding behaviour in large, complex social systems, such as social media platforms and peer-to-peer online communication, is not one of them. This is regardless of what the vendors tell us.

Chapter 6
Children and biometrics

Any parent of a child in a UK secondary school will be familiar with the enormous bundle of paperwork that arrives just before the start of Year 7, when a child transfers from his or her primary to the secondary phase of education. There will be things like uniform lists, health information and permission forms to fill out. And for nearly all of these schools, in this bundle there will also be a fingerprinting consent form, so that children can access school lunches and libraries.

It's rather strange when you think about it. A technology originally designed for tracking criminals during the 1870s is being used in the context of schooling for something as trivial as getting a school meal or borrowing a book for homework. These systems have been pushed hard by the commercial sector, sold as the solution to a variety of societal problems. Obesity? Use our biometric lunch system and parents will be able to track what their children are eating, leading to a reduction in body fat. Reading levels a bit low? Use our biometric library system and teachers will be able to track what children are reading, leading to improved educational outcomes. Classroom behaviour a bit tricky for teachers to manage? Use CCTV during lessons and see if children's heads are pointing in the right direction and their eyes are tracking the teacher. Exams difficult to invigilate? Track typing pauses and eye movements digitally to see if someone is supposedly cheating.

The naivety implicit in these assumptions is just staggering, and the claims are based on no proper evidence whatsoever. Instead, the real reasons these systems have proliferated in UK (and to an extent US) schools are more worrying. In this chapter we explore the past, present and possible future of children's biometrics, and make a case for their immediate eradication in almost all situations. In this respect we take a position very similar to that of the French and German Governments, especially in relation to each country's interpretation of the new European General Data Protection Regulation, which arrived in May 2018, setting new standards for privacy in personal data. In this chapter we'll also include examples of young people's personal views of biometrics in schools, from our work with focus groups of school pupils, as well as the published research literature.

Defining biometrics

First of all, we need to refine what biometrics really are. The most common form is the fingerprint, but the field is developing rapidly and it is possible to track all sorts of measures based on the dimensions and form of the human body, as well as the way it behaves. Biometrics in the broadest sense of the word include the following:

- DNA sequencing
- Visual biometrics of ears and eyes, such as iris or retina scanning
- Finger or hand geometry
- Voice patterns
- Gait analysis (walking patterns)
- Odour recognition
- Behavioural biometrics, for example handwriting or typing patterns, facial expression and posture
- Vein recognition systems such as palm vein readers.[163]

Incidentally many of these work unreliably for young people (the younger they are, the less likely it is that they have a distinctive fingerprint or face shape, as their bodies are underdeveloped in that sense, which is

---

163 In contrast to something fixed like a photo of a fingerprint, this kind of
     biometric can be associated with what is known as 'liveness' tests, that
     demonstrate biometrics as they happen, with all the minute variables
     that take place in the human body being tracked at the same time. So it
     is possible to track a pulse, for example, and map this across the unique
     pattern of veins in a human hand to make measurements more precise and
     individual.

one reason children can't usually use ePassport gates[164]). Many of the measures can be spoofed to some extent, although this is easier for some biometrics than others. If someone has the time or inclination, printed photo masks, contact lenses, digital images, gelatine fingerprint copies and marker pens are all possible ways of subverting biometric access systems with things people might have ready access to. However, most school pupils don't really have the time or inclination, so we won't dwell on spoofing here (plus we don't want to make it too easy for them).

The rise of behavioural biometrics

Digital proctoring
In addition to school meals and library books, and occasionally admissions, biometrics are being introduced for new purposes. In Pakistan, biometrics systems have been introduced by the World Bank to combat fraud in school funding, where public money is claimed for 'ghost' or fictitious teachers, depriving existing schools of the money to which they are entitled. This is a use of biometrics we can feel sympathetic towards, something the Biometrics Institute, the leading industry body, might call 'appropriate use'.

However, the biggest trend at the moment is using biometrics for the purpose of verifying identity in the case of online assessment processes, via digital invigilation systems for examinations, and we perceive this as more of a problem. The practice is more commonplace in a further or higher education context than schools, with uptake increasing significantly since the Covid-19 pandemic.[165] An EU-funded research consortium[166] has carried a large-scale enquiry into this area of

---

164 The other is the need for enhanced human review by a border guard, as part of a process of screening for international child abductions and trafficking.

165 Selwyn, N., O'Neill, C., Smith, G., Andrejevic, M., and Gu, X. (2021) 'A necessary evil? The rise of online exam proctoring in Australian universities.' *Media International Australia*, April. www.doi.org/10.1177/1329878X211005862

166 Adaptive trust-based E-assessment System for Learning (TeSLA) – a 7 million euro project led by Universitat Oberta de Catalunya (UOC) involving a consortium of 17 European Organisations.

biometrics use, in particular how keystroke, facial recognition and voice recognition technologies can be used to ensure that the person studying or sitting an online examination is who they say they are, and whether or not they are cheating. During the Covid-19 pandemic this research has become increasingly topical as examination centres are closed and examinees are required to sit examinations remotely.

Typically the process for digital proctoring involves asking examinees to show the examiner the room they are sitting in for the purposes of the examination via some sort of online tour, as well as demonstrating the integrity of the equipment used, via a live remote link. The examinees are then required to submit to a range of live behavioural biometric measures, which might include things like eye and keystroke tracking, or posture analysis, which are then used to determine whether there are any irregularities taking place. This kind of behavioural biometric is based on the assumption that it is possible to track eye patterns reliably to determine different forms of engagement with the text or screen, and/or it is also possible to associate typing patterns or the way people are sitting with forms of dishonesty. In addition to surveillance by human invigilators, working behind the scenes to assess the probability of cheating are also artificial intelligence tools that have been trained on a population of people quite different to the person being examined, so the potential for false cheating alerts is significant. For example, we know that people with dyslexia may have different patterns of eye tracking movements than the general population,[167] and we also know that many dyslexics of above-average intelligence have not always been formally diagnosed, as they have managed to find workarounds for things like reading which mask their dyslexia.[168] If the artificial intelligence tool underpinning the biometric hasn't included many dyslexics in its training population (perhaps because there is a tendency to train commercial tools on a fairly

---

167 Franzen, L., Stark, Z., and Johnson, A. P. (2021) 'Individuals with dyslexia use a different visual sampling strategy to read text.' *Scientific Reports*, 11(6449).

168 This paper describes the phenomenon in a very readable way. See Holmes, L. C. et al. (2021) 'Developmental dyslexia and compensatory skills: The man who could not read but learned to fly.' *Asia Pacific Journal of Developmental Differences*, 8(1): pp. 143-171.

homogeneous group of people loosely involved in the research project or organisation, plus assorted members of 'friends and family'), then it is going to struggle with identifying the normal eye tracking patterns of people who have non-standard approaches to reading. The same goes with typing patterns and conditions such as dyspraxia (otherwise known as Developmental Co-ordination Disorder) and even simple things like mild Repetitive Strain Injury or other hand, arm and wrist problems.

The EU TeSLA study we mentioned above has tried to address this anomaly in its research sample. The sample included 22,941 learners (including 861 students with special educational needs) which means that 3.7% of the population had some kind of disability or specific learning difficulty. This is a good step in the right direction and is vastly superior to many commercial Ed Tech development efforts taking the quick and dirty 'friends and family' population training approach. But even in the large EU study sample, there are still probably not enough people with non-standard situations. Given what we know about the prevalence of diagnosed and undiagnosed learning difficulties and different forms of disability within the general population, you might expect the figure to be higher than this for a system to be completely robust.[169] What this means for examinees and students is that there is likely to be an inbuilt risk of bias in the way that the artificial intelligence is being used, with a small proportion of users not being treated particularly fairly. This is nothing new, and represents a notorious bias problem in artificial intelligence systems generally.

For example, if 1-2% of users are treated unfairly by a system, that might not sound like very many, but taking something the size of the EU study sample, that could mean an additional 2000 or so users have potentially not been registered by the system properly. That's just about OK for things

---

169 It is hard to pin prevalence down precisely across whole populations, but we know that it could well be higher than 3.7% from looking at studies such as this one of Spanish university students, which estimated a prevalence of between 1.6% and 6.4% of students with dyslexia alone. See López-Escribano, C., Suro Sánchez, J., and Leal Carretero, F. (2018) 'Prevalence of developmental dyslexia in Spanish university students.' *Brain Sciences*, 8(5): p. 82.

like mid-term tests, where there are not many consequences in terms of final assessment grades. However, for higher stakes tests, such as those for university entrance, degree examinations, or online language tests designed for citizenship application purposes, there are really significant consequences if providers don't get this right, and the problem scales up fast to make life difficult for an awful lot of people. So for example, taking the example of secondary school students taking GCSEs in the UK, a 1% bias against specific learning difficulties in future digital proctoring systems would be equivalent to a huge group of approximately 470,000 exam candidates experiencing problems (which would have similar impacts to the use of the controversial 2020 A-level results algorithm in the UK. It awarded grades that worked statistically at a national level, but which ended up being extraordinarily inaccurate at a local level in some cases. For example, some candidates were given a 'U' grade (unclassified), which is only usually given if someone fails to turn up to an examination or fails to write more or less anything on the examination paper, just because someone in their school failed to turn up to an examination within the last three years. The system would decide the bottom ranked candidate in their school in 2020 ought to be given a U in reflection of that event, even though it might have been a strong cohort and normally the candidate might have expected something like a C, allowing them to get the grades they needed to take up a university place. It is rather like being told you have automatically failed your driving test because three years ago someone else had an epic diary fail and didn't show up on the day, and then having your car keys confiscated for a year).

We also know from other studies[170] that if you are in a group that experiences discrimination in one artificial intelligence context, then it is likely other artificial intelligence systems will be biased against you, so the end result is that everywhere you turn, your life will routinely involve more friction and hassle than other people experience, who represent a more predictable fit with artificial intelligence models. The best recorded example of this has been bias towards black citizens in biometric systems involving digital images, which have often been

---

170 The UnBias Project being the most notable, see https://unbias.wp.horizon. ac.uk

trained on predominantly white populations and consequently struggle with different ethnicities.[171] Ultimately, as artificial intelligence is rolled out for more and more purposes within society, getting it wrong has bigger and bigger consequences. The consequence of this is that the use of behavioural biometrics and other surveillance techniques can make examinations very stressful, as students feel they are under scrutiny all the time with no respite, and with little recourse if they are accused of cheating unfairly.[172]

Behaviour management systems

Another significant trend in education is the adoption of digital classroom behaviour management systems. Typically these are a combination of teacher-generated information, for example data on homework completion rates, test scores and disciplinary infractions, combined with images and films of children working at school that parents can logon to and see remotely. These data are reported to parents via an online platform, which they are expected to check regularly as a means of supporting their child's schooling. Looking cheerful and engaged with your learning is what matters here, whether you feel it or not. From a snapshot of (surprisingly frank) reviews on the company website of one example of classroom management software, ClassDojo, teachers seem to speak highly of it. For example:

'Class Dojo is a wonderful program to connect students and teachers. We love the notifications and ease of communication.'

'My students love to earn points and work hard to earn rewards and praise. The parental connection is great and enables parents to see and understand how their child is behaving throughout the day.'

'As a teacher Class Dojo has been a wonderful tool to incorporate into the classroom. It creates a fun and well behaved class.'

---

171 Perkowitz, S. (2021) 'The bias in the machine: Facial recognition technology and racial disparities.' *MIT Case Studies in Social and Ethical Responsibilities of Computing*, February.

172 The phenomenon and associated privacy concerns are described quite well in this article: www.theverge.com/2020/4/29/21232777/examity-remote-test-proctoring-online-class-education

'I love that I can easily reward students for doing what they are supposed to be doing. It is also a great way to communicate with parents.'

Parents, on the other hand, seem less enthusiastic.

'It is her main form of communication so sometimes important info is missed because it is mixed in with a ton of **** **** I get tired of sifting through. It has become time consuming.'

'You have to pay money for them to do anything on it. You can add home stuff which seems odd and not sure how any of that works.'

'The app once a student behaves negatively sometimes makes the student behave in an even worse way as that child knows others know how they have behaved.'

'One possible bad thing is if one child falls behind they can feel demotivated. Children can also develop bad bragging habits on children they are ahead of.'[173]

There are significant privacy implications for children when behaviour management systems like this are used in school, particularly when children are encouraged to compete for behaviour points which are then displayed publicly to other classmates and their families. The endless dashboard-orientated predictive monitoring and nudging that results from this form of data collection can be very wearisome, and add to the time and headspace burden of busy parents, as described in the software reviews. There are also issues surrounding how much autonomy children and parents have in approaching learning if literally everything is being measured, rooted in erroneous links between behaviour and learning that are unproven. Another factor is the level of accountability within such systems – how far is it reasonable to take the teacher's snap judgement as valid, and what happens if a database is built up of these snap judgements that is inaccurate or unreasonable, which then follows a child throughout his or her school career? Do parents and children have the right of appeal or correction? What kind of digital governance

---

173 Capterra. (2021) *ClassDojo reviews*. Available at: www.capterra.com/p/124446/ClassDojo/#reviews (Accessed: 12 August 2021).

measures are in place? This is all serious enough, but it is when machine biometrics are introduced to such systems that we start to see serious problems developing, in terms of digital privacy, as well as accuracy.

In China such an approach has been trialled by the Hikvision Digital Technology company, who installed cameras in classrooms at Hangzhou No. 11 Middle School in 2018. The aim was to use facial biometrics to track different emotional states, including happy, sad, angry, surprised and neutral. The system would then notify the teacher as to whether individual children were paying attention in class. Not to be outdone, Xiaoshun Central Primary School in Jinhua City, went a step further in 2019 and put Star Trek-style headsets on children to track their brainwaves during class. The devices had been developed by the US firm BrainCo, in collaboration with the Zhejiang BrainCo Technology Co Ltd, founded by a former pupil of the primary school. Parental objections were significant and the devices were withdrawn from the school soon afterwards and banned by the authorities.

The problem with systems such as these is that the research on relationships between facial expression or brainwaves and emotional biometrics is not particularly robust, and accuracy levels are therefore relatively poor, so they can easily be misinterpreted. There are also consequences to running what are, in effect, forms of social credit systems in institutions such as schools, where every minor behaviour is digitally scrutinised to generate some kind of score. This can have a chilling effect in the classroom as the range of acceptable behaviours becomes increasingly narrow and restricted, in order to conform to the expectations of a standardised digital system (for example, never glancing out of a window or looking into the middle distance, faking a smile to simulate engagement, and resisting creative or humorous forms of classroom interaction in case these receive a penalty). There are also serious considerations regarding the danger of data breaches, as school systems are frequently relatively poorly protected from hackers compared to, for example, health- or finance-related databases. Comments on the Chinese social media site Weibo at the time expressed exactly these types of concerns in relation to both initiatives. Interestingly, similar classroom surveillance systems have not been rolled out at any significant scale since the original trials. This is probably much to the disappointment of commercial developers, who no doubt sensed an almost bottomless pit of public finance to be drawn upon when selling such systems to every school in the world with a reasonable broadband connection.

The spread of biometric use in schools

The most significant motivation for the adoption of biometrics has probably been the commercial push to provide them. Schools have been a very easy market for fingerprint biometrics in particular, and it was estimated that as early as 2011, 2000 schools in the UK were using them – about 40% of secondary schools overall.[174] In addition, 2000 primary schools were using them, which is about 10% of the overall total. That means roughly 1.28 million of the UK's children were fingerprinted at that time.[175] In the US uptake has most likely been somewhat lower, but it is still significant. The organisation Technavio estimated 24% of US schools would have adopted the technology by 2019,[176] despite the fact that states such as Arizona, Illinois, Iowa, Maryland, Michigan and Florida have banned their use for pupils. There is more resistance to their use outside the US and UK; for example, in Germany they are banned outright in such contexts, and in France there have been legislative moves to minimise their use after the organisation 'Group Against Biometrics' engaged in activism that involved smashing palm readers in schools in 2005.

The reason why their use has become so widespread in the UK in particular relates to accountancy practices. Since the introduction of the 1988 Education Reform Act, and what is known as 'Local Management of Schools', financial autonomy is commonplace. Many schools hold their own budgets and are at liberty to spend it on any technology systems they wish, with little oversight. The motivation here for buying into biometrics systems is reduced administration costs, frictionless reporting, destigmatising of children being given free school meals, and

---

174 Darroch, A. (2011) 'Freedom and biometrics in UK schools.' *Biometric Technology Today*, 2011(7): pp. 5-7.

175 Big Brother Watch. (2014) *Biometrics in schools: The extent of biometrics in English secondary schools and academies*. London: Big Brother Watch.

176 Technavio. (2015) *Biometrics market in the United States in education sector 2015-2019*. London: Technavio.

convenience for pupils (not having to remember a swipe card). When combined with the aggressive marketing tactics of providers, this makes for a somewhat feverish seller's market. To give an example of how this plays out in real life, we've seen one primary school cancel swimming for a number of year groups in order to pay for a biometric system in its modest school library, a room in the centre of the building with no external access. To us, this seems like the tail wagging the dog in school management terms.

However, the price for such apparently streamlined systems is what Andrew Hope has described as 'the silent, continuous and automatic monitoring of an individual's everyday life'.[177] The problem with background monitoring such as this is that an individual citizen doesn't have much scope for redress, for example if a biometric database is stolen and fraudulent identities are built up by reverse-engineering the algorithms that are used to encode the information (fiddly, but not impossible). It also has the effect of priming the younger generation (and their parents) so that they think it is normal and reasonable to be asked for their biometrics for all sorts of mundane uses, even if this comes at the cost of swimming lessons. This may not be a particular problem now, but as biometrics begin to be more widely used, with more serious consequences than denying someone a school meal, then it might be in the future. That was one reason why in 2010 the Director General of the European Union's Directorate for Social Justice raised strong concerns regarding the use of biometrics in UK schools, in a formal letter to the UK's Permanent Secretary, which is a pretty serious diplomatic manoeuvre for something that seems on the surface to be such a minor, day-to-day occurrence. Indeed, more recently, the European General Data Protection Regulation (GDPR) has identified using children's fingerprints as a specifically risky thing to be doing.[178] Therefore, it's

---

177 Hope, A. (2005) 'Panopticism, play and the resistance of surveillance: Case studies of the observation of student internet use in UK schools.' *British Journal of Sociology of Education*, 26(3): pp. 359-373.

178 ICO. (2021) *What is special category data?* Available at: https://ico.org. uk/for-organisations/guide-to-data-protection/guide-to-the-general-data-protection-regulation-gdpr/special-category-data/what-is-special-category-data/ (Accessed: 25 August 2021).

clear that biometrics are not usual or conventionally accepted in a global context with regard to schooling, and the UK and US, and to some extent China, represent something of an exception to the norm in allowing them to proliferate. We are out of step with the rest of the world.

In addition to school funding issues, here are a number of secondary reasons for the expansion of biometric use in UK and US schools over the last decade or so. These are growing school size, issues relating to power and control, and biometrics used as a kind of proxy indicator to show schools as being modern, efficient places. We'll deal with these each in turn.

Growing school size

Over the last half century, UK and US schools have grown significantly in terms of the number of pupils they educate, which in turn has involved a substantial degree of social restructuring. In the US, for example, the proportion of schools with over a thousand pupils grew from 7% in 1954 to 25% in 2004, doubling during the period 1989-2009.[179][180] UK schools have followed a similar pattern, and the average secondary school now has 910 pupils.[181] This has allowed for economies of scale, where schools can offer a broader range of subjects and a greater number of facilities such as laboratories, sports fields, and so on. However, a number of academic studies (we've counted eight, but there may be more)[182] have shown that schools with more than 500 children at primary level, or 900 children at secondary level, can be more difficult to manage effectively. When schools get this wrong, it can have a negative impact on children's

---

179 Leithwood, K., and Jantzi, D. (2009) 'A review of empirical evidence about school size effects: A policy perspective.' *Review of Educational Research*, 79(1): pp. 464-490.

180 Nguyen, T. (2004) 'High schools: Size does matter.' *Study of High School Restructuring*, 1(1): pp. 1-7.

181 House of Commons Library. (2017) *Social Indicator 2625: Schools and class sizes in England*. London: House of Commons.

182 For a list with references see Leaton Gray, S. (2018) 'Biometrics in schools.' In: Deakin, J., Taylor, E., and Kupchik, A. (eds) *The palgrave international handbook of school discipline, surveillance and social control*. London: Palgrave.

education, particularly in areas that are relatively deprived. It is large schools such as these that are quick to adopt biometric systems, which changes the way children's identities are monitored in a school situation. Things start to become more impersonal.

What concerns us here is the risk to the quality of relationships between pupils, teachers, library staff, administrators and lunch supervisors as this process unfolds. A good school is one where (among other things) every pupil is recognised as an individual, and people know your name. If this is replaced by an electronic system that determines what you can and can't have, or whether you are cheating, face-to-face interactions reduce over time, and are themselves replaced with a submission to a remote authority that you can't see and probably don't really understand. In this way, the indiscriminate use of biometrics risks reducing the personal knowledge that adults in the school have of children in their care – something that we think sets a dangerous precedent. Some schools cope with this very well, of course, through the use of houses, schools-within-schools, sections, and so on, but this is not always the case.

In fact, things can be something of a mess in terms of respecting children's privacy rights. Our focus groups have showed us that children and young people don't have a very sophisticated understanding of how biometrics work at all, or the problems they might encounter, for example if the school system confuses them with someone else (although they do find that irritating). We know many young people don't trust biometric lunch cards from some of the comments that have been made when we were talking to teenagers about the real-life experience of using biometrics in school.

'*Sometimes it doesn't work and you have to say your name and year,*' one said.

'*I put £5 on mine but it was only showing £1.50 because someone else had been able to spend my money,*' said another.

'*I put money in my account and then other people put money in my account by accident as well,*' reported a third.

The question is, of course, why are they encountering problems? It's because schools can choose how to set something called a *False Accept*

Rate and *False Reject Rate*, a setting that tells the system what to do if children's fingerprints are very similar (and as we have explained, many of them are, because children's fingerprints aren't as distinctive as those of adults). This is not always calibrated as well as it might be. In any school with a thousand pupils, something like 20-30 pupils may be regularly confused with one another and unfairly told off because of it, thanks to schools and parents not realising this is a normal feature of cheaper biometric systems that only use a limited number of data points.

Being confused with another pupil is just the start of it. It's possible to log into systems and see what your children have been eating. This can lead to some very fraught conversations at home. For example, if a child drops his or her lunch tray, or is perhaps tripped up (this is school, after all, where everyone is not as nice to one another as they might be in an adult canteen), this means he or she will have to buy another lunch. According to our focus groups, this can lead to people being accused of being greedy by their parents. The reverse can also happen, if a pupil genuinely doesn't fancy much for lunch. 'My mother has a "little word" with me if I eat jelly and no lunch,' reported one girl wryly. Now this puts us in a difficult position as authors who are also the parents of teenage children. We have to support the idea of ensuring children have a proper lunch, and Sandra has certainly had the 'If you're going to just have a panini you might as well take sandwiches from home and save £2.20' argument with her offspring. On the other hand, we are supposed to be preaching the gospel of children's data privacy rights, a conflicting imperative if there ever was one.

In addition to issues of surveillance and confusion surrounding biometrics used for school lunches, young people invariably have no idea how long their data are stored for, where this might be, and who might have access. Apart from the day-to-day annoyances described above, they are fairly indifferent to any related privacy problems (as we might expect given their age and experience). They see biometrics systems mainly as a convenient tool. Awareness has changed a little since our first research into attitudes towards biometrics in 2006, but not as much as we might have hoped.

We have also found in our work with head teachers and school governors that instead of a personalised approach to privacy, biometric systems are sometimes adopted fairly uncritically. As we have mentioned above, in the types of rudimentary systems used in schools, fingerprints are converted to ten or twelve data points, which is not a particularly high level of encryption, but head teachers and governors in our research do not seem to interrogate providers about this and demand something more robust for their money. It's the same with access systems that use facial biometrics for all visitors to a school. Similarly, little guidance is given on data storage, and many machines are relatively accessible. We found in one case that a school was using a generic 'library user' login to access its biometric system, and the provider had not given advice on why this might be a bad idea. In some of the schools in our focus groups, they had even started taking the systems out because they were proving to be so unreliable. Clearly thousands of pounds had been invested in something that wasn't working in some schools.

Despite this, we saw that some governors are quick to make sweeping comments about the use of biometrics being acceptable, based on very little other than the hackneyed phrase 'If you've done nothing wrong, what do you have to hide?' Pupils saw their use as cool and a bit sci-fi, also saving them the bother of remembering library and lunch cards. Parents were divided, with most not really thinking through the biometric issue, assuming that if the school condoned it, everything was fine. We are hoping that since the introduction of GDPR things have become more considered and mindful, but our feeling is that it is probably time to run another research study to find out whether changes in legislation have resulted in changes in attitude towards biometrics and data privacy.

Power and control

The French sociologist Michel Foucault (1926-1984) talked about power in a useful way that helps us understand some of the ways it is deployed in institutions. There are different forms of power and the one that interests us here is something he classified as 'disciplinary politics'. This is the idea that schools control groups of pupils in order to achieve a particular objective. This is not the same as dominating a group with the motive of subjecting them to something they might not want or like. Sometimes you need to have rules and structures simply to be able to organise everyday life, and this is the disciplinary process going on at school.

As schools grow in size, what is known as the 'family meal' with children sitting around a table served by an older member of the school, becomes more and more difficult to organise. Cafeteria-style meals become the preferred option. In this way we see a kind of urbanisation going on, which involves fewer social interactions and an increasingly depersonalised approach to eating. As part of this process, children change status from young people taking part in a social or communal eating activity, into individual consumers fuelling themselves for the afternoon ahead. Their relationship with the school cafeteria is also financialised.

For the academic, there is an interesting question here about whether this shift is neutral, and whether it matters. The jury is out on that. The French philosopher Jean Baudrillard (1929-2007) would probably see this act of consumption – school dinners bought using biometrics – as neutral and not worth making a fuss about. On the other hand, sociologist, anthropologist and philosopher Pierre Bourdieu (1930-2002) might see consumption dictated by taste and social class (explaining why some parents insist on sending their children to school with packed lunches, because they regard school meals as insufficiently nutritious, or why they ask for swipe cards for their children instead of allowing them to be fingerprinted, being more privacy aware). However, one thing is clear, and that is that in something as mundane and simple as school meals, we see within-group differences start to emerge among parents that are quite separate from any considerations to do with whether someone has free school meals or not. The introduction of cafeteria systems, and more specifically the use of biometrics, make a significant contribution to that.

Looking modern and efficient
In the UK and the US, almost all schools are part of a competitive system whereby they need to make sure they seem attractive to parents, in order to ensure that school choice works in their favour. In the UK in particular there have also been extensive attempts to modernise the school estate over the last two decades or so, and it is in this context that we see biometrics used as an adjunct to interior design. As Golborne High School reported in its newsletter in 2016:

'The old canteen was plain, boring, colourless and wasn't a very nice place to eat in as there was mess everywhere, drinks spilt, etc. However the new canteen is a nice environment to eat food in. In has brightly coloured benches, vivid colours, and more space on the benches to sit with your friends. The pictures on the wall make it look modern and classy. Pupils and teachers can now pay with an image of their fingerprint on a scanner, called biometrics, making the canteen look even more posh and much more efficient as pupils are not having to find the correct money to pay for things.'

Newsletter, Golborne High School, 2016

Some of the companies involved in the sale of biometrics systems to schools have complicated relationships with procurement systems. Recently Sandra looked into the commercial aspects of a Private Finance Initiative (PFI) involved with a state-maintained primary school in Paisley, Scotland. In a PFI the buildings are refurbished or replaced by a commercial organisation, and then leased back by a local authority over a period of something like 25 years. This can be very expensive for schools, and the success of the programme varies greatly.

This particular primary school installed a very high-level biometrics device in its dining room, in the form of a palm-vein reader, something more fitting as part of an access security mechanism for a nuclear installation rather than a means of having young children choose their pasta and yoghurts. This installation was part of an extensive modernisation programme carried out by Amey PLC. This firm had a partnership with Glasgow City Council to develop several schools with a £100m build value, and they worked with Yarg Biometrics and Fujitsu to develop new technologies suitable for sale to schools as part of this project, presumably as a way of further leveraging the contract for additional value. In other words, children and their schools became the guinea pigs for new technological devices, something which appears to have been paid for by the taxpayer but with any potential profits going to the companies concerned. Yet this was all seen as something exciting and new, rather than intrusive and inappropriate for low-level use such as school meals. As the managing director of Yarg Biometrics said at the time, 'The kids love it. It is the whole James Bond thing'. To paraphrase Mandy Rice-Davies, well they would say that, wouldn't they?

The future of biometrics in schools

Is this what eating is now all about? Shuffling along the lunch queue of life, giving away your personal data in return for some fish fingers on a tray? Or are there different forces at play here? It's obvious that views on biometrics in schools are polarised. On the one hand, they are seen as a fairly straightforward technological development that speeds up school lunch queues or makes classroom management easier. On the other, they represent a significant invasion of privacy and something of an identity battleground for those pupils easily confused by the system. We think it is important to step away from these arguments, however, and take a different view of what is happening. There are some more important questions to ask.

1. **Are schools are getting too big?** If they were smaller, you wouldn't need so many control systems to track people and keep an eye on their behaviour. When we look at the research on school size, it often talks about the impact on academic achievement, but it doesn't say very much about what it feels like to attend an institution that resembles a medium-sized airport along with 1500 other adolescents and associated teachers and auxiliary staff. As adults, very few of us work in organisations as large as this, in such a regimented way, so it makes sense to consider whether it's as suitable for children as we once thought. We're not alone in having these concerns. The Human Scale Education Movement[183] was founded by British educationalists in 1985, and there is a parallel US movement in the Coalition of Essential Schools.[184]

2. **What does knowing a child really mean?** A task sometimes given to trainee teachers is to follow an individual child around for a day, and occasionally it's found that some children don't have a single conversation with anyone, even though it might appear they are part of the melee that is the school classroom and corridor. Schools work best when everyone knows who individual children are, and when they have a chance to express themselves. This could well mean maximising the human and minimising the digital,

---

183 www.humanscaleeducation.com
184 www.essentialschools.org/

particularly as we move to greater use of Artificial Intelligence systems. We think it's much more valuable for a school meals supervisor to engage with individual children about what they are eating and why, than to leave it purely to a digital system to monitor and control at one remove. (Looking ahead, that supervisor should not be a robot, by the way.) The same applies to classroom teachers seeking to maximise learning, or schools and colleges trying to make sure their examinations are properly invigilated and fair.

3. **Should cafeterias be replaced with dining rooms?** If we really care about children's food consumption and social development, meals should probably take longer and be taken in mixed-age groups with some sharing and leisurely conversation as part of the process, to bring back the human touch. Martha Payne, a schoolgirl from Scotland, highlighted a few years ago on her blog *Never Seconds*[185] quite how bleak the contemporary school meal on a plastic tray can be, and how magnificent they are when the food is shown a bit of love. Looking ahead to the future, if we want to tackle issues such as food security, obesity, and social belonging, we need to think very hard about addressing the decline in formal communal eating that has taken place over the last few decades.

4. **Should we be more grateful for what we are about to receive?** There could usefully be less choice about what to eat at school, which would save money and speed up the more boring parts of the school lunch process, rendering some aspects of biometrics redundant. This means offering one meal for more or less everyone, a strategy which worked for schools for decades. St Christopher school in Letchworth, UK, has gone completely vegetarian, which is a good way of simplifying menus as well. The MUSE school in Calabasas, California has gone further and provides vegan meals. If the nutritional content is suitable, this provides a useful solution to diverse dietary needs.

5. **How valuable is reading compared to book curation?** If a child occasionally forgets to return a library book, this may be

---

185 Payne, M. (2014) *Never Seconds*. Available at: www.neverseconds. blogspot.com/ (Accessed: 13 August 2021).

a price worth paying for having old-fashioned lending systems, perhaps even honesty-based ones in small schools, instead of fingerprinting everyone and chasing books digitally through automated reminders. Librarians (where they still exist) should be allowed to adopt the policies they think promote reading to best effect in their schools, not have biometric systems imposed on them by the school administration.

6. **Are we teaching or incarcerating?** We haven't discussed attendance systems in the chapter to any great extent, largely because the research data is limited to the technical advantages of biometrics in this context, with little reflection on the social context. They also tend to be used in post-16 and post-18 systems. However, it occurs to us that, if you have to use biometrics with young adults to track why they aren't in post-compulsory education, perhaps you'd be better off talking to them about why they don't want to come in. It may be that you need a different offer.

7. **What is the price of modernity?** Looking modern does not necessarily mean you are a better school. If schools are buying biometric systems, they need to be asking about the impact they are likely to have on pupil attainment, engagement and welfare. If there isn't any hard evidence, then it's time to consider whether there might be unintended consequences. (One of these might be hygiene issues, as biometric platens tend to end up being rather grubby after a day's use. Scientists at Purdue University tested platens in 2007 under clinical conditions and declared them to be no dirtier than your average doorknob, with bacteria dying after 20 seconds on devices. However, in schools it may be that more children would touch the platen within that time frame than we would expect to touch a doorknob. We also note that the Purdue team didn't test for things like threadworm – otherwise known as pinworm – egg transmission, something endemic within schools.)

8. **How are we defining good behaviour?** There are dangers in a future that promotes a desired model of behaviour based simplistically on keystrokes, eye tracking patterns, voice recognition and postural aspects, simply because this is easy to measure by computers using artificial intelligence machine learning systems. It can

result in high levels of surveillance of the human body that is little more than a kind of 21st century phrenology, grounded in weak science that is being oversold to educational institutions. It also risks causing a great deal of day-to-day stress among learners, as they are never sure about when they are being watched, and how this is being analysed and interpreted. The algorithms that make decisions about their behaviour are opaque, and children and their parents also potentially have only very limited rights of appeal.

In summary, we think biometrics should be reserved for serious life-or-death situations, such as access to industrial installations and anti-terrorism initiatives. If they are dumbed down for use in school for more trivial functions, and trained poorly in a machine learning sense, then they become much less exceptional and valuable. This risks adverse social and ethical consequences, as well as future security problems as people lose control of their own biometric data. If we are going to use people's bodies as an identity token, or derive high stakes behaviour measures from the way they interact with machines, then we need to be much more thoughtful about the way we do this.

Chapter 7

Beyond the fourth industrial revolution: Artificial intelligence and education

We sometimes hear the term 'fourth industrial revolution' in the media. By this, we generally mean artificial intelligence being used to facilitate many day-to-day commercial functions, ranging from deciding what you might have to pay for an airline ticket, to deciding whether a firm is prepared to sell you health insurance (we can tell how this is done via various patents that are regularly published, which give the game away). There are even systems that can decide with a relatively spooky degree of accuracy whether you are likely to develop diseases such as cancer or Alzheimer's in the near future. Data mining, speech recognition used by financial organisations for security purposes, and military applications, such as analysing drone recordings, are also examples of artificial intelligence in action.

In the field of education, we see simpler artificial intelligence tools used to help children practise maths skills, via online software systems such as the *Mathletics* package many UK schools subscribe to, or to practise modern foreign languages online via a package such as *Language Perfect*. Publishing companies such as Pearson are investing heavily in larger-scale systems that have the potential for systematising and individualising education globally for millions of children. The idea is that using these tools is supposed to make life, or learning, easier, cheaper, and more effective.

However, in contrast, artificial intelligence is regularly presented in the media as either apocalyptic or disruptive, and it is here we fall back onto science fiction analogies. One common example in use is the HAL 9000 computer in the film *2001: A Space Odyssey*, in which the computer decides at one point it is in its best interests to kill off the spaceship crew in order to continue with its programmed directives. 'Open the pod bay doors, please, HAL,' commands crew member Dave over and over again. HAL goes very quiet, and finally responds, 'I'm sorry Dave, I'm afraid I can't do that … I know that you and Frank were planning to disconnect me'. Films like this teach us to mistrust machines on the grounds of their lack of humanity. Stephen Hawking's comments on artificial intelligence didn't help. 'The development of full artificial intelligence could spell the end of the human race,' he announced, in a BBC interview in 2014.[186]

In the light of this, the main question for us regarding artificial intelligence and education is primarily a philosophical one. How do we reconcile the enormous power of artificial intelligence systems with our fundamental need to retain our humanity wherever possible? This is a complicated problem, and so far developers have not experienced a great deal of success. Here are a few examples of where the relationship between humans and machines can go very wrong.

AI taunting

Trumpington Community College, a brand-new secondary school in Cambridge, England, has been designed as a cutting-edge facility, with every technological tool in there that could reasonably be managed. Classrooms are fairly open-plan and flexibly-sized, paper is more or less absent, and tablets and laptops are in abundance. Perhaps the most innovative development is the virtual school cat, known as Cinder.

This particular moggy was designed by London studio Umbrellium,[187] and is designed to amble across the school's networked screens at will,

186 BBC. (2014) *Stephen Hawking warns artificial intelligence could end mankind*. Available at: www.bbc.co.uk/news/technology-30290540 (Accessed: 16 August 2021).

187 Umbrellium. (2016) *Case study: Engage students in energy and sustainability*. Available at: https://umbrellium.co.uk/case-studies/ trumpington-community-college-augmented-bms/ (Accessed: 31 August 2021).

pausing perhaps to engage with groups of pupils. Her direction can't be controlled. Pupils might play with the cat on the augmented reality screen in the main foyer, or if the cat gets tired, she might pop up on one of their laptop screens. The pupil can then 'feed' the cat with the amount of food being determined by how much energy has been generated by the school's solar panels. The aim is to get pupils interacting with the technology around them, and to link the building with their educational activities. In many senses this is quite life-affirming and future-orientated, in the sense that it's possible to get a glimpse of an environmentally-aware future. However, a group of local teenagers from another school was heard discussing it, and it's clear that they had a darker, more immediate interest in the project.

'I know what we would do with it,' said one. 'We'd try to starve it to see what would happen. Because that's more fun.'

It takes you aback to hear something like this after you have been basking in the warmth of a pleasant vision of tomorrow's youth using technology to be environmentally aware. However, this wasn't an isolated experience. Some months later, Sandra was attending the 2017 summer conference of the Leverhulme Centre for the Future of Intelligence, where leading researchers in a diverse range of fields were attending events and being encouraged to fraternise. This was located at Jesus College, Cambridge University. Sandra spent a bit of time in one of the breaks watching Pepper, a semi-humanoid robot manufactured by SoftBank Robotics, who is supposed to be able to read emotions. She was initially impressed. Robots in education have come a long way since the early 1990s when Sandra first encountered plastic turtles being programmed by nursery children to roam around the room and play little tunes, via the programming language Turtle Logo, (developed in 1967 by a small team of three US developers, and reasonably common in tech-minded schools by the 1990s).[188] Pepper does quite a bit more than that, and gets around a great deal. A version of Pepper has even visited a Parliamentary Select Committee in the past, and answered questions about Caresses, an

188 Abelson, H., Goodman, N., and Rudolph, L. (1974). 'Logo Manual.' *Artificial Intelligence Lab, Massachusetts Institute of Technology.* https://dspace.mit.edu/handle/1721.1/6226

artificial intelligence system aimed at assisting with care of the elderly.[189] Anyway, conference delegates were chatting with Pepper and asking questions about directions, weather and so on. Sandra even asked the robot to pose for the obligatory selfie.

Pepper and Sandra in summer 2017

Then Sandra noticed the mood changed a little. Someone started to tease the robot and deliberately tried to confuse it. Its innocence and its confusion brought the onlookers up short, and people shuffled away. The fact the robot didn't know it was being teased seemed to make them uncomfortable.

---

189 UK Parliament. (2018) *Pepper the robot appears before Education Committee*. Available at: https://committees.parliament.uk/committee/203/ education-committee/news/102507/pepper-the-robot-appears-before- education-committee/ (Accessed: 16 August 2021).

In both examples, there was a clash of the technological and the human, with humans being compelled to assert their superiority over the technology in some way. The same happened when Twitter introduced an artificial intelligence chatbot designed by Microsoft called 'Tay'. Within 24 hours, Twitter users had managed to teach the chatbot how to be racist. Not completely racist, but fairly nasty, nonetheless.

Screenshot of Tay, ingénue chatbot developed by Microsoft – live for 16 hours from 23 to 24 March 2016 before being taken down

Digital privacy rights

It's clear that humans and artificial intelligence systems, whether entirely virtual like Cinder the cat and Tay the chatbot, or humanoid like Pepper, co-exist uncomfortably at best. What does this say about the future of the curriculum? It says two very important things. First of all, we know that humans like to sense a degree of control, a degree of agency, over many things in their lives. Recently Sandra was working with colleagues in Germany, where researchers were talking to local young people about their views of telecoms infrastructure, digital privacy rights, and internet personalisation. Almost all of them told us that they wanted more transparency from providers, and more say in the design and infrastructure of the internet generally, ranging from broadband and 4G availability in their areas to what advertisements they were shown. They wanted to know more about the information kept about them by providers, and to be able to opt out of things they were uncomfortable with.[190]

This translates in a very interesting way to the school curriculum indeed. In the light of very many group interview conversations with young people over the past decade, we have proposed the following digital curriculum for schools, which we think should be woven into existing subject provision. These bullet points represent the missing links in the modern school curriculum as far as preparing the next generation for a digital adulthood is concerned. It also says something useful about how parents could and should approach digital issues in the home.

- **Privacy, information and education rights**, including understanding of the new European General Data Protection Regulations. Young people need to have high quality conversations with the adults around them about what this means, and parents need to be careful not to share too much personal information about their families online, especially given the proliferation of the Internet of Things, with digitally enabled devices collecting vast amounts of personal data, but not always storing it appropriately. Indeed, this has been the thrust of recent work carried out by the UK's Children's Commissioner, culminating in the report we mentioned earlier, *Who knows what about me?* published in November 2018.[191]

- **Management of time and space**, so young people use digital tools mindfully. Sometimes this might even mean putting away the computer and going outside, or meeting friends in real life when they can. It also means parents putting away their own mobile phones, tablets and laptops, and setting a good example. In 2017 King Alfred School in Hampstead organised an internal conference entitled 'The Adolescent and the Phone', to discuss such issues, as well as whether mobile phones should be banned in

---

190 See Leaton Gray, S., Mägdefrau, J., and Riel, M. (2021) 'Life in the digital slow lane: How deprived young people are set up to fail.' *British Journal of Educational Studies*.

191 www.childrenscommissioner.gov.uk/publication/who-knows-what-about-me/ (Accessed: 20 November 2018).

school.[192] This is an example of home-school best practice, in the sense that adults are getting together to find bespoke, considered solutions to the problem of an 'always-on' culture. France has gone even further and banned mobile phones in schools nationally. Perhaps we should consider that in the UK and US?

- **Provision, maintenance and protection of digital infrastructure**, so that as young people grow into adults, we are preparing them to be the commissioners and caretakers of large-scale systems of the future. It is perfectly possible for schools to have a computer committee of young people to discuss provision in school, for example, so that technology is something children and young people are involved in at a different level from just being end consumers. If handled correctly, they can bring insights about the real-life deployment of technology at school, which might mean that systems can develop to be cheaper, more cost-effective, and better protected. In this way, school council work can spread well beyond its more common remit of dealing with issues surrounding uniform compliance, tuck shop arrangements and corridor discipline discussions.

- **Digital criminology**, so society has a better understanding of the risks and limitations of technology when it is used for bad purposes. One particular area where young people need to be careful is the risk that they be targeted by fraudsters in relation to pupil loans, as reported in the UK's *Financial Times*.[193] Schools can help anticipate situations such as this by explaining typical scenarios, how they can be prevented, and what can be done if a young person is the victim of a crime, including the importance of good communication with parents and the authorities, if the worst should happen.

- **Digital citizenship**, so there is a better appreciation of the potential for inclusion within society. As in the work with German

192 www.kingalfred.org.uk/Reflections-on-KASS-Annual-Conference---The-Adolescent-and-the-Phone (Accessed: 30 November 2018).

193 Greenlagh, N. (2017) 'Student loans company targeted by phishing scammers.' Available at: www.ft.com/content/b7a60f30-9232-11e7-bdfa-eda243196c2c (Accessed: 30 November 2018).

colleagues we discussed earlier, it is not just about whether you pay for a good quality broadband or 4G/5G connection. Whether someone has an equal involvement in a digital society can also be subject to external issues, such as the scale and spread of local technology infrastructure. Young people in poorer areas (which companies can work out from IP addresses and type of connection used) may be paying more for less, with associated impacts on their educational journeys as accessing certain resources becomes more difficult and complicated for them than for other young people in more affluent areas. It is important that this is challenged.

• **Digital consumption**, so young people are able to become more discerning, and recognise aggressive advertising when they need to. We have found in fieldwork with young people that those who use their phones mostly for educational purposes seem to receive the most education-related advertisements, for example, advertising relating to courses they might like to do, or university open days, whereas those young people who use them primarily for shopping are generally denied those sorts of invitations. This may well influence engagement with lifelong learning generally.

• **Respect, consent and empathy**, so collaborative, interactive use is a positive rather than a negative experience. Researchers such as Danah Boyd, Principal Researcher at Microsoft Research,[194] Professor Jessica Ringrose, professor in the Sociology of Gender and Education at the UCL Institute of Education in London, and Professor Sonia Livingstone, professor of Social Psychology at the London School of Economics,[195] have done significant work on the shift in ethics and morals taking place with the young in relation to how they interact online. They have written about the emergence of new forms of consent, for example, in the way pictures are shared. Many young people seem to consider that if something is exchanged digitally, further permission needs to be sought if it is handed on

---

194 Boyd, D. (2014). *It's complicated: The social lives of networked teens.* New Haven: Yale University Press.

195 Ringrose, J., Harvey, L., Gill, R., and Livingstone, S. (2013) 'Teen girls, sexual double standards and "sexting": Gendered value in digital image exchange.' *Feminist Theory*, 14(3): pp. 305-323.

further. This is a form of morality that has emerged spontaneously from the lived experience of using the internet and social media, rather than something that has been imposed externally.

- **Legislative protections**, so the boundaries of the law become clearer, and hopefully allow us to avoid a repeat of electoral interference scandals, where there were accusations of behavioural biometrics being used to nudge voters inappropriately during the Brexit referendum, for example. So far, the development of the internet has been commercially led to the extent that the law is lagging a long way behind. This is not sustainable in the modern economy as it has a corrupting effect on the ability of citizens to enjoy control over their own lives, as well as to participate democratically to the fullest extent. There are subsidiary problems surrounding the general ownership and control of the internet and its platforms, given the centrality of them to everyone's lives in the 21st century, and it's here where anti-trust laws in the US, and similar anti-monopoly and anti-competition laws in other countries, can kick in and protect the public.

- **Media as an information source and influencer**, so young people can demonstrate discernment over what they are told, and understand when it might be propaganda or 'fake news'. We found that young people have been fairly confused about the quality of the supposedly 'factual' information they receive, although they are increasingly aware they need to be sceptical. The UK Government has been quite proactive here, calling for expert evidence and publishing recommendations in relation to 'fake news', for example.[196] More high-level initiatives such as this need to be carried out, if we are to promote honesty and civic values online.

---

196 House of Commons Digital, Culture, Media and Sport Committee. (2018) *Disinformation and 'fake news': Interim report*. Fifth Report of Session 2017-2019 London: House of Commons. Available at: www.publications. parliament.uk/pa/cm201719/cmselect/cmcumeds/1630/163002.htm (Accessed: 20 November 2018). Our written expert evidence is linked to here: http://data.parliament.uk/WrittenEvidence/CommitteeEvidence.svc/ EvidenceDocument/Culture,%20Media%20and%20Sport/Fake%20News/ written/47380.html

- **Wellbeing and mental health**, so young people understand the importance of protecting themselves from the adverse consequences of a digital life. This is a complex problem as there may not be an obvious cause and effect pattern. However, widely publicised 'hygiene factors' already exist, which can be transferred to the context of digital engagement. These include things like keeping physically active, staying in touch with people face-to-face, and appreciating yourself rather than arbitrarily comparing yourself unfavourably to others. Social media sites such as Instagram are somewhat problematic here, as young people are frequently relatively unaware of the intense level of artifice that goes into creating professional shots, and the invisible financial support that goes into promoting lifestyles through paid posts.

The list above represents a useful curriculum for a productive and healthy digital life, that can be adapted for use at home, and is a way of ensuring young people experience an appropriate degree of agency and control over their internet use as systems become more complex and interlinked, influencing the furthest reaches of our lives. There is another aspect to the role of artificial intelligence in society, however. The second issue we need to bear in mind is the centrality of the human condition to our society. It is not enough to leave all our decisions to machines and just be told to shrug it off when things don't go our way, for example if we experience discrimination at the hands of a remote algorithm deciding whether we can, or cannot, have something. We need to use the time and money saved through outsourcing some of our thinking to machine learning systems to become even fuller, richer examples of the human condition.

Wet versus dry intelligence

By this we mean revelling in what it means to be messy, imperfect humans with our beautiful 'wet' form of intelligence, as opposed to 'dry' machine intelligence. We have been crafted over millennia by evolution to be unbeatable at so many things, and these abilities should be a constant source of joy to us. These include things like our extraordinary ability to assess with our senses the vaguest and most uncertain forms of probability, such as whether something which looks or smells a bit dodgy can really be trusted or not. We can make the most extraordinary deductive leaps, such as Einstein thinking about the journey of a train through a station and realising that this says something important about the theory of relativity. We can express enormous altruism and compassion, for example when people give their organs or even their lives for others. This is what it really means to be human.

There is only one way that this can be properly manifested, and that is by making the arts and humanities increasingly central to day-to-day life in schools. It is only by engaging with, and reflecting on, the human condition in all its variations that we can understand how we are best able to deploy the age of the machine to our advantage. Rather than being sacrificed on the altar of employability, or cost, over the coming decades, things like music, drama, dance, literature and art need to become increasingly more prominent, alongside the teaching of high-level communication skills and moral and ethical values. In a machine-led world, where so many functions are carried out using algorithms we can't be expected to comprehend personally, we need to hang on to what it really means to be human, and feel able to contest those algorithms when it matters. Only then will there be any real point to education, and only then can we be sure we have prepared our young people for their digital futures.

To this end, we present four alternative scenarios for artificial intelligence and education using a horizon year of 2030. In case you are not familiar with them, scenarios are a type of business modelling technique used to develop innovative ways of thinking about uncertainty, and something Sandra specialised in during her PhD research. A well-written scenario will contain elements of both good and bad, positive and negative, and in groups of four they cluster particularly well. Not everything in a scenario will turn out to be true, of course, but somewhere within the thinking will be unexpected and possibly disturbing aspects. The idea is that everyone is able to reflect on the 'What if?' nature of these aspects and prepare mentally for situations which may be very different from things they encountered previously. The oil company Royal Dutch Shell originally developed this process in the 1970s, anticipating the oil crisis, and it's been used regularly by business and industry since, so it's a tried and tested approach.

Four alternative futures for artificial intelligence and education

Alfie

Alfie is sitting in his space at the Woodcote Community Learning Centre feeling rather hungry, swinging his legs in eager anticipation of a hot dinner and a run through the play yard. He has worked his way through the new maths tasks and he is really pleased, because he thinks he has at last got to grips with the simulated science experiment, as well as finally learning his seven times table properly, but he definitely would like some food. His machine hasn't bleeped yet, though, so it probably hasn't worked out how he is feeling, meaning it is out of step with his biorhythms again. This has happened before, and his mum has come in to speak to the school administrators about sending him for lunch late. Alfie looks around the room and notices all the other children have gone already, and he is the only one there. He decides to sneak out anyway, pressing the 'Away' button on his workstation first. He can always make up the time at the end of the day. When he gets to the lunch pod, there isn't much left to choose from, so he selects the tofu fritters again. He doesn't really like the tofu fritters, but it's not the worst option. If you get in early, they have things like sweet potato fries, but that has only happened to him once. While he is on his way the sole of his shoe starts flapping about. The tape has come off, and it's annoying him as he walks towards the school yard. Alfie decides that running is probably not a good idea, so he strolls towards the buddy bench, where he sees Jacob, another boy from his learning group, sitting and watching the other children as they finish their games and pack up their balls and ropes. Jacob is a couple of years younger than Alfie and they often meet on the buddy bench. They have a lot in common because they are both at a similar stage of their learning on the computer system, and they both get out for lunch late most days. The boys have a chat about football, which is the first conversation they have had with another human being since their parents dropped them off at the learning centre that morning. The sky darkens; they look up and notice the first rain drops falling. The boys decide to head back to the computer block for another few hours' work.

Bella

Bella has fallen out with her friend Lilly during the drama lesson. They were working very well on the improvisation project together with the other girls, and then suddenly things went bad when someone accidentally hit someone else with their elbow, and it looked like it was on purpose. Lilly's brand-new wool blazer has been slightly ripped near the pocket, and she's worried that means she will get in trouble at home. Work on the project stops completely. The electronic tutor trundles up to the group and asks what is wrong. Both girls try to explain their side of the story at the same time, with a lot of hand waving and pointing, and occasionally raised voices. The electronic tutor tries to make sense of the accounts, but it is no good. There isn't enough data. The drama teacher is electronically paged and comes over to take charge of the situation. She calms the group down and patiently listens to each member explain what happened, from different points of view. Bella and Lilly are quieter now and look at each other, each trying to judge what the other one is thinking. The teacher beckons the electronic tutor over again and asks it to replay what it saw happening in the drama improvisation. The angle isn't very helpful, so that information doesn't get the group anywhere, but the teacher points out that Bella and Lilly have been approached negatively by the electronic tutor more times that term than any of the other young people in their class, and suggests that they need to work on their relationship skills. She sets them to work together, helping a group of younger pupils on the other side of the room. Bella and Lilly shuffle reluctantly to the group as instructed. They don't see the point of this, and it means they can't finish their improvisation exercise. It needs to be as good as they can make it, otherwise their grade average will fall too far. This could have a bad impact on their applications to college later on, as their files will go through a machine-based sift based on a grade average before they end up with a human admissions tutor. This makes them very nervous about school in general. Meanwhile, the drama teacher flags up their files on the learning system, so that they are invited to attend a group discussion at lunchtime about peaceful co-operation in the drama studio. Relationships matter a lot at St Hilda's school.

Carter

Carter is on a mission to complete the entire Winterton Academy middle years syllabus before Christmas, so he can get onto learning more about *DeepSpace*, his favourite computer game, as it is rumoured among the pupils that this is one of the choices when you've scaled the top level of the usual tasks. He is thinking of becoming a games designer when he leaves school. What he doesn't realise is that the computer system has great plans for him in terms of its personalised learning offer, and after he has finished the cross-curricular project on the Babylonians, he is going to be introduced to the history of mathematics and its early relationship with cuneiform script. Despite trying to resist, Carter is completely drawn in and before he knows it, he is calculating proficiently using factors of 60 and special tables, and recording this in a rudimentary manner on a virtual clay tablet. The afternoon passes very fast with him watching breath-taking reconstructions of Babylonian life in high definition, rotating 3D representations of museum objects and archaeological finds, listening to simulations of early Babylonian musical instruments, and logging into a real-time, live-streamed film of some new work on the Babylonian archaeological sites, taking place right then and there in modern-day Iraq. The system even allows him to have a couple of screens open at once, a rare treat at school, so he can keep an eye on the excavation as it happens. It's important not to miss any exciting moments when finds come out of the ground, after all. He also spends time practising different calculations until he masters the Babylonian mathematical process. Just before home time, the screen bursts into life with virtual confetti, and Carter is invited to see some cuneiform clay tablets for real in the British Museum the following day, sharing a driverless car with three other pupils sharing similar educational trajectories and interests. Carter is pleased and cross at the same time. He gets a great trip but yet again his plan to explore the deepest recesses of *DeepSpace* at school has been sabotaged.

Daisy

Daisy is sitting in the head teacher's office with her parents and the school's Special Educational Rights Co-ordinator, and everyone is looking very earnest. It has been a long day. The head teacher is showing them some graphics on the tabletop display. The system has picked up some problems that have come about after Daisy's earlier bout of the Covid-19 virus, by comparing her progress to the typical trajectory of other female final year pupils of the same chronological age and genotype nationally, who have contracted the same disease, since March 2020. The system has already adjusted Daisy's learning path and exam entries in response to a reduced timetable during the last couple of months, on account of her chronic tiredness. Now it wants to go further. It is suggesting that her ability to focus on studying is in the bottom 10% of her recovery group nationally, and that this figure is likely to fall further in the coming weeks. This means that the adjustment isn't working sufficiently well, and that further steps are needed. It has mapped a new course of study against the times of day when Daisy seems to be at her most alert. It has set the duration carefully according to the latest published evidence on mitochondrial dysfunction that comes about in relation to post-viral fatigue, impacting negatively on energy levels. The system has also alerted the local family doctor and occupational therapy service that Daisy will need a review in the next fortnight. As it may take some time for the other services to respond, due to a local outbreak of influenza and associated additional pressures on health facilities, it has also suggested that Daisy takes the next week off school to attend a teen 'long Covid' intensive therapy group at the local hospital, and a referral can be triggered as soon as the family gives consent, along with transport and follow-up services. Despite the bad news, Daisy feels relieved. She knew something wasn't right.

Chapter 8
The future

As one might expect with this sort of topic, it never stands still. There is frequently a demand from a journalist for our time or comment on the latest online safety or online education issue, and they usually want to know where the harm or benefit is. We also see emerging technologies adopted by society in ways we could never have predicted, or world events bringing unexpected changes to our lives that involve significant changes in the way we use technology to best effect. This includes innovations like behavioural biometrics and artificial intelligence, networked learning environments and social robots, wearables and mobile tracking technologies, and the use of Big Data underpinning everyday processes and actions through automated decision-making (and all the problems that brings, as we have described). This digitalisation of the mundane aspects of everyday life has many facets. As we have argued throughout the book, not all of the developments are negative, although sometimes they can be if they are not approached carefully or democratically enough.

Covid-19 and lockdowns

At the time of writing, we are about (all being well) to emerge from the latest English lockdown, caused by the Covid-19 pandemic. Over the last 15 months, lockdowns in the country have driven much of working life, education and social life online. Digital technology has been a boon for keeping in touch, communicating outside physical meetings, and maintaining at least some level of education during what were inevitably challenging and difficult times. Digital technology has clearly been invaluable, and many of us are now far more familiar with the online meeting or classroom than we used to be. Teachers have generally excelled themselves in this regard, rapidly shifting to new online pedagogies that allow greater diversity of provision and practice than ever before.

However, the Covid-19 lockdowns have also, unsurprisingly, brought about a great deal of concern around children's online identities and attendant safety issues. Surely, goes the standard narrative, if they're online a lot more, they are more at risk of harm from grooming, coercion, exploitation and abuse? This makes sense on a superficial level – if children are online more, the risk will increase in proportion with time spent online. We have seen, across the safeguarding sector, many people making claims that we should be more concerned, due to the increased exposure to online risk.

During this time, we have also had many conversations with schools and pupils who do not share this view. Young people have pointed out that their *social* activity online hasn't increased that much. After eight hours in online classes, they generally took the view that they wanted a change from the online world. While digital technology was undoubtedly the means with which they maintained relationships and kept in touch with friends when they were unable to see them, they did not feel that they were more at risk, or that the internet had become the sole focus of their personal identities.

However, if we explore the response of the safeguarding community, we do get a window into the language of yet another online moral panic. While we don't doubt the genuine concerns of organisations wishing to be alert to the potential for harm as a result of lockdown, we can also see the inaccuracy of the language beyond the headlines. As an example, we can consider a number of articles from the sector [bold in quotations in this section has been added for our emphasis]. Firstly, from the NSPCC:

> *'Young people with digital access are spending more time using social media and online resources: this increases the risk that they **may** experience online-facilitated grooming or other online harms, during a period when demand for online child sexual material is **known** to be on the rise.'*[197]

---

197 NSPCC. (2020) *Isolated and struggling.* Available at: https://learning.nspcc. org.uk/media/2246/isolated-and-struggling-social-isolation-risk-child-maltreatment-lockdown-and-beyond.pdf (Accessed: 16 August 2021).

While it was unquestionable (if we explore, for example, Europol[198]) that demand for, and the exchange of, Child Sexual Abuse Material (CSAM) did increase during lockdowns, there is less confidence in the statement that children are in fact at more risk as a result. The deliberate use of 'may' rather than 'will' unpins a lack of evidence to support the claim. While it might be expressed with the best of intentions, the ambiguity of language highlights that this is conjecture, rather than fact. If we consider the above-mentioned report by Europol, which does show an increase in the exchange of CSAM, it is again rather the *possibility* of children being more at risk of harm as a result of lockdown, because they had received reports that calls to children's safeguarding helplines (for example, the NSPCC's Childline) had increased:

'Teenagers in particular contacted the helplines more frequently and increasingly via electronic means instead of phone calls. It is important to note that contacts are about a range of different issues, with child sexual abuse-related matters being only one of them.'

It is interesting to note that while they state calls and contacts have increased, they cannot provide evidence that this is due to online harms.

They also raise concerns around Self-Generated Explicit Materials (teens sending each other nudes), and again provide an unproven statement:

*'The increase in the level of material being shared and the amount of SGEM being produced **may** lead to an increase in sexual coercion and extortion in the near future.'*

UNICEF also put out a briefing to raise their concerns around online harms during lockdown,[199] again with language that implies risk, rather than confirming it:

---

198 Europol. (2020) *Exploiting isolation: Offenders and victims of online child sexual abuse during the COVID-19 pandemic.* Available at: www.europol.europa.eu/sites/default/files/documents/europol_covid_report-cse_jun2020v.3_0.pdf (Accessed: 16 August 2021).

199 UNICEF. (2020) *COVID-19 and its implications for protecting children online.* Available at: www.unicef.org/media/67396/file/COVID-19%20and%20Its%20Implications%20for%20Protecting%20Children%20Online.pdf (Accessed: 16 August 2021).

'It is highly likely that COVID-19 will heighten this risk to children, as highlighted by national law enforcement agencies and civil society organisations around the world. Spending more time online may increase the likelihood that children come into contact with online predators.'

And finally, WeProtect, a global public–private partnership between governments, NGOs and private companies,[200] also released a briefing report[201] on the impact of Covid-19 on online exploitation:

'Greater unsupervised internet use means children are likely to be exposed to greater risk of sexual exploitation online, including sexual coercion, extortion and manipulation by offenders. Exchange of self-generated material is also likely to increase, as children are now experiencing most of their social lives only online.'

Given the gravitas of the organisations releasing this information, it is unsurprising that many in the sector, and those who have children, were concerned, particularly given that the headlines that went alongside them (for example 'Impact of Covid-19 on child sexual exploitation and abuse online'). However, we were seeing little evidence of this being borne out in reality. While we had observed the level of conjecture in the language used, we could see that there was a lot of interest and concern so, as academics with a penchant for measuring things and looking for evidence, we served a Freedom of Information request to all local authorities to provide a breakdown of safeguarding disclosures (safeguarding concerns reported by schools, police, members of the public, etc) per week during the pandemic, to see if disclosures about online harm were increasing. Another factor in doing this was that in a study Sandra was leading, which explored children's transitions to secondary school during the Covid-19 pandemic, there were some isolated reports of schools making additional safeguarding referrals

200 WeProtect are 'the only international public–private partnership dedicated to fighting child sexual exploitation and abuse online', comprising of government, industry and NGO representatives. (www.weprotect.org)

201 WeProtect. (2020) *Impact of COVID-19 on child sexual exploitation and abuse online*. Available at: www.weprotect.org/library/impact-of-covid-19-on-child-sexual-exploitation-online/ (Accessed: 16 August 2021).

as a consequence of the experience of vulnerable families during the pandemic, and domestic violence, so we wanted to see if this played out online as well. While we are still examining the responses in detail, the top-line finding[202] is that there have been no increases of statistical significance in relation to online safety. What many in the sector expected to happen did not occur. But we would ask whether feeding the moral panic stoked the fears of parents and added undue stress to the family home as a result.

The Online Safety Bill

Generally speaking, regulation has been running behind technological development during the time we have been researching this area. In drawing our book to a close, there are two other aspects of online safeguarding we feel are worthy of mention. The first of these is the Online Safety Bill, which has been recently released in draft form[203] and is the crowning glory of the government's goal to make 'Britain the safest place to go online in the world'. While we would not encourage readers to have a look at the full 145-page draft (as we have!), it does illustrate, once more, government thinking on what safety looks like online. At the heart of the bill lies the concept of 'duty of care' for online service providers. It is down to them, and here the bill is clear, to make sure citizens in the UK are not exposed to illegal material and what is also referred to as 'legal but harmful'. How 'legal but harmful' is defined in law remains to be seen. However, it is clear that companies that cannot demonstrate duty of care will be found liable for abuse that happens on their platforms, however legally and ethically complex this becomes.

However, again, there seems to be little attempt to define or delineate whether this aligns with the broader legal concept of duty of care, and its relationship with what in civil law is referred to as tort of negligence. Is the duty of care in the bill being defined as related to a form of

---

202 Phippen, A., and Bada, M. (2020) *COVID lockdown and online harms.* Available at: www.cambridgecybercrime.uk/COVID/COVIDbriefing-13.pdf (Accessed: 16 August 2021).

203 https://assets.publishing.service.gov.uk/government/uploads/system/uploads/attachment_data/file/985033/Draft_Online_Safety_Bill_Bookmarked.pdf

negligence? If so, how might the company be able to demonstrate due diligence or protect itself from vexatious or unsubstantiated claims of harm? Negligence is the subject of much legal debate and is certainly not getting any less complex, as can be seen in the language used by ˙Markesinis and Deakin in their defining text on Tort Law:

> *'The experience of the last thirty years or so if anything, suggests a dialectical process of evolution with many, often inexplicable, tergiversations.'[204]*

If the government is introducing failure to protect from online harm as another form of negligence for which one might make a civil claim, we might expect a level of detail in proposed legislation such that companies might understand the incoming legislative requirements on their content monitoring and technical interventions (as this is fundamentally all they can hope to do).

We also note that, in a 145-page bill, there are a mere two mentions of 'education', where it states the appointed regulator – Ofcom – should:

> *'...carry out, commission or encourage educational initiatives designed to improve the media literacy of members of the public.'*

There is still a long way to go before we see this bill reach Royal Assent, and we are sure there will be much to debate. However, it seems clear from the phrasing that there is to be a focus on an absence of harm, which is perhaps not the most progressive of positions. Certainly, companies need to provide tools to ensure that people can report abuse, and block those causing it. They also need to show they are mindful of the ages of service users. But it is difficult to see how they can usefully play a part as the ultimate moral guardians for all 'lawful but harmful' content, as this concept seems poorly defined and subjective in interpretation. Perhaps this phrase will be dropped from the final bill.

Ofsted report into sexual violence in schools

Finally, just as we were putting the finishing touches to this book, the inspectorate of schools and colleges in England – Ofsted – released the

---

204 Deakin, S. F., Johnston, A. C., and Markesinis, B. S. (2012) *Markesinis and Deakin's Tort Law.* 7th ed. Oxford: Oxford University Press, p. 99.

results of their review of sexual abuse in schools.[205] This is certainly worthy of comment in terms of exploring critical thinking and response in this area.

Triggered as a result of the many thousands of harrowing testimonials of pupils on the website Everyone's Invited,[206] the inspectorate sought to investigate the scale of sexual abuse in school settings. Unsurprisingly for those of us who work in the area, they discovered that much sexual harassment and abuse in schools is 'normalised' and that much of this harassment takes place online, with comments about how girls can be asked many times a day to send nudes, or that social media accounts were set up with the sole intention of harassing someone. In the BBC reporting of the release of the report,[207] the head of Ofsted said she was shocked at the findings, and the inspectorate has now essentially mandated to schools that they need to accept this activity goes on and they need to work on how to tackle it.

While the report, and coverage, is to be welcomed, it once again shows the lack of learning from history. We have shown, in chapter 4, that there has been work in the area of sexting for well over 10 years. As far back as 2012, Prof Jessica Ringrose and colleagues from the UCL Institute of Education produced a report for the NSPCC[208] that explores these issues of normalised sexual abuse in detail, making a number of recommendations for schools. In 2016, the Women and Equalities Select Committee conducted an inquiry and produced a detailed report with recommendations[209] on this topic too. So, for senior people in the education setting to be 'shocked' to discover a piece of work in 2021 has similar findings to a report in 2016, which had similar findings to a report in 2012, is a concern, as it shows that we are not responding to

205 www.gov.uk/government/publications/review-of-sexual-abuse-in-schools-and-colleges/review-of-sexual-abuse-in-schools-and-colleges
206 www.everyonesinvited.uk/
207 www.bbc.co.uk/news/education-57411363
208 www.researchgate.net/publication/265741962_A_qualitative_study_of_children_young_people_and_'sexting'_a_report_prepared_for_the_NSPCC
209 https://publications.parliament.uk/pa/cm201617/cmselect/cmwomeq/91/9102.htm

the evidence we have. Clearly sexual assault and harassment in schools is a sensitive and difficult issue to address, and we can appreciate that it might not be something that generates headlines or political momentum, but we have known it goes on for a long time. We would hope that given the volume of testimonials on Everyone's Invited, and the findings of this new report, that schools will now be mandated to provide clear routes for disclosure, education around these issues, training for staff and effective, scrutinised policies, so that pupils who have been abused can report it and be confident they will be listened to, believed, and supported.

Is there hope?

In this book we have explored the relationship between digital technology, childhood and children themselves. We are mindful that we can sometimes paint a bleak picture of how young people are supported in living their hyperconnected lives, and we know some of what is presented in this book might be overwhelming and make parents feel that it is almost impossible to keep up. However, while this has been a varied exploration, covering topics as diverse as AI, sexting, tracking, biometrics and ghost stories, there are a number of key themes that permeate all of our discussions:

1. Don't panic! Most of the time, most young people are using digital technology safely and for positive reasons. However, that is not the sort of headline that will sell newspapers and generate traffic to their websites and, moreover, it is not the sort of message that will generate many donations to NGOs and charities.

2. Being online is not the same as crossing the road. While we might talk about road safety as a concept, applying that to the online world is problematic. The road setting tends not to change too much, and crossing the road is a relatively straightforward operation that can be addressed with simple safety instructions. In contrast, there are always new aspects to the online world, new games, apps, platforms and devices. We have to bear that in mind when talking about risk. There will never be one fixed solution that always works.

3. The very word 'safety' implies protection from danger, risk or injury. The logical conclusion is to assume the only way we can

keep children free from risk online is to take them offline. We doubt they will appreciate this, and all it means is that they might find their way to different types of harm in the offline world – remember the dangers of the back garden trampoline in our Parental Anxiety Calibration Tool! What we can do is provide them with information on the types of risk that exist online, what they can do about them and, more importantly, if they do feel at risk, they can tell you without fear of being told off.

4. Technology is not the solution, but it can provide a set of tools to help mitigate risk. As we have discussed at length, technology cannot prevent harm – tools for monitoring or tracking children don't mean they are safe, they just mean we can see the harm occurring or, more likely, the children will bypass the tools and hide their activities anyway. However, technology can provide a number of tools if we are aware of them and are confident they can help. Blocking and reporting are fundamental parts of most mainstream platforms and if we know how to use them, they are useful tools in harm reduction and risk mitigation.

5. We can see much of the theory of moral panics being applied to most online phenomena. They are new and unfamiliar; therefore, they must be harmful, yes? And this is not helped when, as soon as any new digital innovation hits the mainstream, the mass media's view is 'How will this cause harm for children?' Before we respond to a moral panic, it is important to take a breath, do some fact-checking, and maybe speak to some young people. While that friend on social media might be sharing a concern about a new app that is causing harm to children with the best of intentions, a panicked response can ultimately result in children being exposed to something they weren't aware of. Simple messages such as 'If you see anything online that is upsetting, tell us' is far more measured than 'Have you heard of <new digital phenomenon x>, it's making children self-harm?!'

6. There are no easy answers. Child safeguarding is something that is done with a whole community of stakeholders – parents, schools, sports coaches, community workers, police, technology providers, etc. Speak to your children's school about what they do around

these issues. Who do you speak to if you are concerned about something? What are their policies on this sort of thing? Engage with others who educate, help, and support your children. You don't have to do everything on your own.

7. Listen, don't judge, and understand. Young people want to be listened to and believed if they are worried about something or something has happened to them. They don't want to be told they're just being silly, telling tales or 'That's what happens if you do that'. Young people who are confident they will be listened to and supported are far more likely to disclose harm or worry.

However, perhaps the most fundamental message that weaves throughout our different discussions is the importance of being able to think critically and logically about the issues we face as parents with children in the hyperconnected age. In the digital world, everyone has an opinion. Generally, this is based upon personal experiences with digital technology, underpinned by whatever angles the media (and social media) wishes to cover. This *digital unconscious bias*, which we all bring to these issues, needs to be something we are aware of and can acknowledge. As parents, our immediate response to any new concern is to protect our children and ensure they are safe from harm. To do this, we need to be mindful of the accuracy of what is reported or shared, take a deep breath, do some fact- and source-checking, and maybe even speak to our children about their thoughts and how they think concerns might be tackled. Parents can certainly offer guidance and support in relation to children's digital lives, but they don't automatically know what's best. Where parents can also do some good is to hold providers to account as well. If you think something isn't serving children as well as it might do, it's important to speak up, whether that's because a product is overly commercialised, or inaccurate, or uses an unhelpfully opaque algorithm, or for any other reason. Stakeholder involvement of this type is crucial in terms of achieving robust digital environments that support the social and ethical values surrounding family life.

Finally, we'd like to bring back the quiz from the beginning of the book, this time with the answers.

Quiz

1. How would you mostly define children?

    A. Smaller versions of adults

    B. Vulnerable beings

    C. Innocents, a blank slate

    D. Creatures requiring civilising

    E. A lifestyle choice

Answer – All of these terms are used in different contexts and situations, depending on what people are trying to say. In many ways, definitions of childhood say more about the adults around them than children themselves.

2. How risky is it to be a child?

    A. Things are getting more dangerous for children compared to 1950.

    B. Things are getting safer for children compared to 1950.

Answer – Definitely getting safer, quite dramatically so.

3. Which of these represents the biggest risk for children at the moment?

    A. Online witchcraft sites

    B. Video gaming

    C. Being attacked or abducted by strangers

    D. Obesity

    E. Online pornography

    F. Drugs

    G. Radicalisation

    H. Personal data being stolen

    I. Covid-19

    J. Cars

    K. Back garden trampolines

Answer – Statistically speaking it is cars and back garden trampolines, depending on how you are looking at it. School sport comes pretty close as well, in the high-risk stakes.

4. Which is the most dangerous internet phenomenon?

   A. Blue Whale Challenge

   B. Momo Challenge

   C. Slenderman

   D. *Doki Doki Literature Club*

Answer – None of them. They are all myths (although D is at least loosely based on an app that actually exists).

5. Which has the biggest impact on children's wellbeing?

   A. Eating breakfast regularly

   B. Limiting screen time

Answer – Eating breakfast. Screen time doesn't seem to have a particular impact on children's wellbeing unless it's literally the only thing they do with their waking hours.